CALL ME
Teacher

BY
ELEANOR A. DANIEL

Copyright © 2016 by Eleanor A. Daniel

CALL ME TEACHER
by Eleanor A. Daniel

Printed in the United States of America.

ISBN 9781498478465

All rights reserved solely by the author. The author guarantees all contents are original and do not infringe upon the legal rights of any other person or work. No part of this book may be reproduced in any form without the permission of the author. The views expressed in this book are not necessarily those of the publisher.

www.xulonpress.com

Table of Contents

Dedication vii
Acknowledgments ix
Endorsement xi

Chapter 1   An Idyllic Childhood 13
Chapter 2   On My Own 27
Chapter 3   Go West, Young Lady 35
Chapter 4   A Busy Interim 44
Chapter 5   Lincoln: New Challenges, New
            Opportunities 49
Chapter 6   A Brief Sojourn in Oklahoma City 63
Chapter 7   I Thought Cincinnati Would Be
            Home Forever 67
Chapter 8   Emmanuel: The Place to Be 103
Chapter 9   Six-Year Postscript 126
Chapter 10 Come Travel with Me 141
Chapter 11 Those Slightly Tarnished Golden Years . 183
Chapter 12 Reflections 188

Conclusion 191

Dedication

To the memory of my parents
Donal W. [1911-1997] and
Bernice (Hillig) [1913-1998] Daniel
who taught us the value of hard work,
timeliness, and caring for others

Acknowledgments

A book just off the press is a proud moment for the author. Yet the book is really the result of many voices. With that in mind I want to acknowledge the following voices in this work.
- Ottie Mearl Stuckenbruck who gently, but firmly insisted that I do this.
- Judy Stevens, Ottie Mearl Stuckenbruck, Judy Parmenter, Ann Kelson, and Bruce Parmenter who read the manuscript and made helpful suggestions to strengthen the narrative.
- Bruce Parmenter who wrote the conclusion.
- C. Robert Wetzel who provided an endorsement.
- My sister, Kay Matthews, a professional secretary, who produced the final manuscript.

Endorsement

It would be difficult to imagine how any one person could do more in Christian ministry in one lifetime than has Eleanor Daniel. From service in local congregations to teaching and administrating at the college and seminary level and to cross cultural mission service in countries around the world, her achievement is extraordinary. Her life not only reflects the dynamic history of contemporary Christian Churches and Churches of Christ, she is a living example to the women who are currently preparing for various ministries in our colleges and seminaries. I am grateful that the woman that I knew as Dean Daniel has taken the time to share with us her life of service. She expresses her own surprise that God has chosen to use her as He has. Hence, in her own words, "Only God can orchestrate that." Thank you, Lord, that you did orchestrate it, and thank you that we now have this fascinating autobiography.

C. Robert Wetzel
Chancellor, Emmanuel Christian Seminary

Chapter 1

AN IDYLLIC CHILDHOOD

I was born February 28, 1940, in Detroit Township, Illinois, near the rural hamlet of Milton. Though, of course, I don't remember, it was a threatening world. The Great Depression was past its worst, but full recovery hadn't yet come. Many farm families lived in areas in which no electricity was available; and most ominous of all was the cloud of war that hung over the world, especially as the war expanded in Europe. It wouldn't be long before the United States was in the war—both in Europe and the Pacific.

My parents were Donal and Bernice Daniel. Dad was the youngest son, by several years, of Riley and Nora (Barnett) Daniel; his brother and sister were older than he by a decade and more. He finished eighth grade, but attended not even a day of secondary school. He planned to be a farmer with his father, at least the fourth generation of Daniel men who had farmed in Pike County. (Two more generations of Daniel men and a sixth generation—a grandson named Bauer—succeeded my father.) Mother was the oldest of three daughters born to Lawrence G. and Goldie (Davis) Hillig. She had finished high school and a business course just in time for the depths of the Great Depression. Her primary work experience, rather than being in business, was instead as live-in help for a family.

Donal and Bernice were married December 24, 1935, at the Methodist parsonage in Pittsfield, Illinois. Donal was twenty-four and Bernice was twenty-two. Like many young couples of the time, they lived with his parents for more than four years. Their first child was born in November 1936; a loving child, I'm told, who was the pride of her parents and grandparents. Glenna died in December 1938; her funeral was on Christmas Day, a shadow over every Christmas Day celebrated by my parents for the rest of their lives. Sometime in 1938, my grandfather retired from farming. He and Grandma moved into the village, leaving my parents in the home where they had all lived, and my father doing the farming. I was born in that house in February 1940. (Yes, there was a February 29 that year—but I beat it by about four hours.)

My dad was a warm, caring man with a legendary sense of humor. On one hand, he was eminently patient; he would sit for hours, allowing me to brush and comb his beautiful black hair. On the other hand, he had a frightful temper, administering dreadful spankings when we disobeyed. He taught me to love baseball, and I loved working outside on the farm with him.

He demonstrated his sense of humor in a variety of ways. For example, he had a nickname, often a play on a name or characteristic, for many with whom he had frequent contact—Maggie Mae for Margaret, the waitress at the local restaurant. He called himself the laziest man in his village—he even had a cap with that designation.

An Idyllic Childhood

One of the funniest events occurred one day when our family was on the way to visit Mother's cousin. Dad observed that once we passed the drive-in theater, it would be only a few minutes from our destination. Mother objected, insisting that the theater was beyond our destination. They argued about it for a short time until Dad would argue no longer. A few minutes later Dad slammed on the brakes. Everyone wanted to know what was wrong. "We have to turn around and go back. There is the theater! We missed the town." Everyone howled with laughter—everyone but Mother, that is.

This was their common way of relating. If one said one thing, the other insisted it was something else. Their physician called them The Bickersons.

Mother deeply loved her children, but she, too, had a temper. She was largely humorless; but she was a hardworking woman who worked outside on the farm as needed, and with the chickens and garden. She was a strong disciplinarian and expected her children to be seen and not heard when they were in public.

My sister Jean was born August 5, 1941, again delivered in our home; though, of course, I remember nothing of the event. Then the United States was pulled into World War II in December of that year. Many men the age of my dad were drafted, but he was given a 4F classification—he was a farmer and the major support of his parents.

The family expanded again in September 1944, when my sister Kay was born. This time Mother delivered the baby in the newly opened hospital in the county seat about twelve miles from where we lived. Jean and I had all kinds of names selected for this child should it be a girl—Cookie and Pepsi Cola among them—but none of our ideas won out. Mother and Dad's choice prevailed.

The family was completed in September 1949, when my brothers Jerry and Terry were born. Two brothers—what excitement! Twins—what a curiosity in our little community!

One of the many visitors to see the babies carried in whooping cough. The babies came down with the whooping cough and had pneumonia as well. We three girls got the whooping cough as well, though in a milder form than the babies. Both boys ended up back in the hospital when they were six weeks old, one of them at the point of death. Had they not been big babies weighing 8 ½ pounds each at birth, at least one would not have survived.

It was a stressful time for our family. The babies were in precarious condition, and Mother had to be at the hospital with them. We three girls couldn't go to school and needed attention at home. Our grandmothers helped as they could, and Dad hired a woman to come in to prepare meals, clean, do laundry, and babysit. We survived, but I remember it as a hard time.

The babies were in the hospital a couple of weeks. But they required intense care, even after they got home. My parents talked later about never getting a full night of sleep until spring because the twins had a dreadful cough until it warmed up the next spring. One event stands out.

Our telephone was on a party line. We had been threatened with dire consequences if we were caught listening. But bored with nothing to do, I listened, just in time to hear that one of the Daniel boys was not expected to live throughout the day. And I could not tell anyone but Jean lest the consequences be administered! It added to the stress.

I was reared in a community, in the real sense of the word. People knew, cared, and helped each other. They tolerated, even affirmed, a wide array of personalities. And, of course, almost everyone knew everybody's business. But when needs arose, they responded. A good example is when my brothers were born. The neighbors made sure that the corn was harvested when Dad had to spend long hours at the hospital. And women in the community took care of feeding the harvest crews because Mother too was at the hospital with the babies.

A range of colorful personalities were a part of our immediate and somewhat larger community. There was Otis Denison—Ote as he was commonly called. He was deaf and spoke loudly enough for everyone to hear everything he said, even at great distances. He had strong opinions about the evils of television, especially what watching it would mean for the eyesight of the viewers. When my brothers began wearing glasses when they were in early elementary school, he was sure that it was the result of watching television. Never mind that we didn't have a TV set. Nor did it occur to him that all of the five Daniel children wore glasses early in elementary school!

Then there was Tony Ward who lived in the village. He had a speech impediment and was mentally deficient. He was always present at the little Christian Church in the village and had a very long string of perfect attendance pins for Sunday School attendance. A few people were rather cruel to him, but most people respected him and treated him well. My dad always made sure that Tony had a Christmas gift and served as a protector when some were unkind.

The neighborhood school was at the social center of the community. Few events, other than school programs, were held at the school, but the families attached to the school had many social gatherings.

It was to the neighborhood rural school that I went when I was in first grade. (The school closed after that year, and we rode the bus to the village to go to school from that time on.) We had an older lady as the teacher in our one-room school composed of about twelve students—three first graders, a fourth grader, a couple of fifth graders, two sixth graders, a seventh grader, and a couple of eighth graders.

The school building was a typical country school building: an entry area that served as a cloak room and the large classroom where the first graders sat on the right of the teacher, the eighth graders on the left, and the remainder between. In the back was the coal stove that provided heat during the winter. Outside were two outhouses—one for boys and one for girls—coal shed, and plenty of play space. I lived about a half mile from school and walked to school much of the time.

Though I didn't learn much my first year of school, I loved to attend. In fact, I decided then and there that I would be a teacher. But a major problem presented itself. At the end of first grade, I couldn't read. However, I memorized very well. The teacher read the new material to us a day or so before we were to read it, and I memorized the content. It appeared that I could read very well. But my mother learned the dirty secret in the spring when she expected me to read material from early in the year. But my forgetter had pushed out the memorized material, and I couldn't read it. She was mortified: her oldest child was a dummy. But she went to her first grade teacher, who lived a few miles away, and took in advice and borrowed materials to teach me to read. She did a good job, for in second grade I was placed in an advanced reading group. And I learned to love to read.

An Idyllic Childhood

My best friend all through elementary school was Beth Denison. The Denisons lived about a half mile from us. She had two brothers who were several years older than she. During the summer I was at their house or she at ours almost every afternoon. Although we don't see each other very often these days, when we get together, a part of our shared time is reflecting on those childhood play days.

When I was in second grade, I rode the bus to town to school. The bus came to our house and turned around, loaded the children from our family and those from another family that lived on a dirt road about a mile east of us. Compared to the one-room country school, the school in town was big, with probably 80-100 elementary children and an equal number of high school students—all in the same building.

Two churches were a part of the village—one the dying Methodist Church where I first attended Sunday School and the other the Christian Church. Most of the people I knew attended the Christian Church, if they attended church at all. Out of a dozen families in our immediate vicinity, about a third of them had one or more members who attended the Christian Church; the Daniel girls attended the Methodist Sunday School; the rest weren't in any church at all.

We attended the Methodist Church for only a short time. Mother and Dad didn't attend unless some special children's program was being presented. Although I had a Sunday School teacher who told wonderful Bible stories that I loved, we didn't continue to attend because on most Sundays, attendance included a dozen or so kids and three older ladies. Some of the time two of the ladies were absent. The only adult present on many Sundays was a blind woman, leaving the children to run wild. When

Mother found that out, we no longer went: she expected us to behave and for leaders to be present to make us behave.

Social life was limited. There was a makeshift movie house in town at which movies were shown every Tuesday and Friday night. We often were permitted to attend on Friday night. Dad took my sister Jean and me to town, gave us fifteen cents, and went to the farm implement store to visit with other men in the community. At the movie, the younger children sat in the front; the high school couples sat in the back, often smooching more than watching the movie. After the movie was over, we had a nickel left to buy a candy bar or soda before going around the square to the implement store to find Dad.

The other social outlet for many of the farm youth was 4-H. Two active clubs—one for agricultural projects, the other for home economics projects—were available. Several girls—myself included—were in both clubs.

I joined a 4-H home economics club when I was 10, the earliest possible date to be in 4-H at the time. Mother insisted that I take sewing and cooking. Later I also took canning and freezing projects. I joined the agricultural club a couple of years later, showing registered Black Angus beef and Jersey dairy cattle, raising chickens, and doing gardening.

4-H clubs provided a rather active social life—not just with the projects, but also with county social events, softball teams, and other county events. I did all of them, I think.

I was in 4-H for as long as possible—ten years to be precise. 4-H provided many opportunities to develop skills and leadership. I entered public speaking competitions and one year represented our county in the state public speaking contest at the state fair in Springfield. I was a junior leader, and one year was selected as one of two girls and two boys from our county to attend the state junior leadership conference at Allerton Park near Monticello, Illinois. There we were given leadership responsibilities and attended lectures and classes on leadership. That was a great gift for the future.

Jean, Kay, and I began to attend Sunday School at the Christian Church the spring I was in sixth grade. We were influenced to go by two persistent ladies, my fifth and sixth grade teacher at school and the minister's wife at the Christian Church. The minister had been at the church for several years and was well respected in the community. He hung out at the implement store with the men, creating a real respect for him by Dad who by and large was opposed to preachers and churches. We found a spiritual home at that church. We were introduced to church camp at Lake Springfield Christian Assembly. It was natural that Jean and I accepted the Lord's offer of salvation and were baptized in December 1952.

The long-time minister moved on in a few months and a young, energetic preacher arrived. He developed an active youth program as well as a focused outreach program. It was not very long until Mother started attending church again—she hadn't attended since her marriage. Eventually Dad consented to attend Sunday evening service, and he and Kay were baptized on the same day when I was fifteen.

When I was sixteen, our family moved about five miles north to a farm that my father bought. He had always before farmed on a cash rent basis. This move was in many ways a traumatic move for Dad. He had lived in the same house on the same land from the time he was four years of age until he was almost forty-five.

In some ways little changed when we moved. In other ways, everything changed. We joined new 4-H clubs in the community where we lived. We attended a different church, this time the Detroit Christian Church. The biggest change was that Dad decided he would attend on Sunday morning as well as Sunday evening.

By far the biggest challenge that confronted us, however, was Mother's illness that summer and fall. She had not been well much of the summer and was hospitalized in September. The doctors determined that she had tuberculosis, a disease that generally required about a year-long placement in a sanitarium. It was before the introduction of many of the drugs that later were commonly used to treat TB. Mother was taken to a sanitarium in Springfield, about sixty miles away, and Dad was left with five children to oversee in the midst of his busy life as a farmer. It turned out that Mother was hospitalized just twenty days less than a year.

In many ways, that was a difficult year, but one that called for all of us to work together. Jean and I prepared breakfast and supper. We ate lunch at school, and Dad "made do" as best he could. One neighbor did the laundry for our family of six and her family of five until new neighbors moved in and helped her with the laundry. When summer came, Jean and I did the laundry. (And no, we didn't have an automatic washer.) The church ladies usually brought one meal a week, at a time of our choosing. Farmers helped Dad get the corn harvested so he could make twice weekly trips to Springfield to see Mother. A couple of ladies made clothes for us. Our 4-H leader was a great emotional and practical support. The minister of the church often accompanied Dad to Springfield, an action that solidified my Dad's faith.

I remember being so tired at times during that year that I didn't think I could make it through the day. We got on the bus about 7:10 in the morning to go to school—and didn't get home until 4:00 or shortly thereafter. My brothers were only seven and needed their mother. My youngest sister was twelve in the seventh grade with her first male teacher, and she too needed Mother. Dad was beyond busy trying to farm, taking care of his mother who was in a nursing home, and visiting my mother who was over an hour away and who had to have lung surgery in the midst of her stay. In the midst of it all, his only sister died at age 55 as their older brother had done three years earlier. I'm not sure any of us would have emerged whole had it not been for the church where we found support and care, or if my dad had not insisted that he would keep life as "normal" as possible for us.

"Normal" meant that Dad encouraged us to remain involved in whatever school and community activities we already enjoyed and that we be in church every Sunday. "Normal" meant that when we visited Mother on Thanksgiving or Christmas Day, he found a restaurant where we could have a traditional meal. At Thanksgiving, when we went to the selected place to eat, Dad, Jean, and I were happy to have the traditional turkey dinner, but Kay, Jerry, and Terry wanted hamburgers and French fries! And on Christmas, Dad arranged with Grandma Hillig and my Aunt Vivian to eat our holiday meal in the evening so we could spend the day with Mother.

My mother came home from the sanitarium in early September of my senior year of high school. Now the family had a wide range of other adjustments to make with Mother back and in charge. The balance was achieved, generally successfully.

I graduated from East Pike High School in 1958, as valedictorian of the class. Milton High School and Pearl High School had merged in 1955, with the new entity called East Pike, and met in the building that had been Milton High School. A small high school had its drawbacks: courses were limited with only basic algebra and geometry in mathematics offerings and no languages available. My courses, though, included four years of English, Algebra, Geometry, one year of Home Economics, a year of history, four years of science (including Physics and Chemistry), Physical Education, and five business courses. Each of these courses was a year-long course, leaving us credibly educated, even if we didn't have languages and other course options.

What the small high school lacked, however, was far outstripped by the positives. Almost everyone was involved in some school activity such as sports, Girls' Athletic Association, Future Homemakers of America, Future Farmers of America, yearbook staff, paper staff, or student government. Most of my involvement was with GAA and student government. I served as Student Council president during my sophomore, junior, and senior years. I was the yearbook editor when I was a senior, and I contributed to the school paper during my junior and senior years. Those activities, plus my involvement in 4-H and church, taught me many leadership lessons that proved valuable through the years.

Much of my senior year was focused on where to go to college. I'm not sure why it was such a foregone conclusion that I would attend college. My parents certainly had no expectations that I should. Teachers, however, encouraged me to consider college preparation for work, and, of course, I had that longstanding desire to be a teacher.

The choice of college was not easy. My parents had no money to send me to college; if I wanted to go, I had to figure out a way to pay for it. Scholarships weren't readily available. And my interests had turned to teaching in the church. My academic preparation would likely need to be in a Bible college—and none of them were regionally accredited at the time. That caused a certain level of consternation by teachers. And any possible scholarships would not be usable at an unaccredited school.

After considerable emotional struggle and plenty of prayer, I chose a Bible college—Lincoln Bible Institute in Lincoln, Illinois. There I could major in Christian education while being assured that I could attend one of two or three schools after graduation where my degree would be accepted and I could get teaching licensure.

All too soon the generally idyllic world of my childhood and youth came to a close. It was time to move to Lincoln to go to college.

My parents Donal W. and Bernice (Hillig) Daniel

My siblings and I from left to right: Terry, Jean, Eleanor, Kay, Jerry

Chapter 2

On My Own

I arrived on the Lincoln Bible Institute (now Lincoln Christian University) campus in August 1958. My parents took me to school with just about everything I owned in one suitcase. And I was out of the nest, on my own for the first time.

LBI was a small school of about three hundred students when I arrived. It had been established in 1944, by Earl C. Hargrove, the president, who was also the minister of the Lincoln Christian Church when the school was founded. The school had met in rented facilities for a year or two, then in a downtown building near the church structure. By 1958, however, the school was on a campus on the east side of the city, the site it currently occupies. Only a few buildings were on campus: an administration/classroom/library building, another building with classrooms (later expanded to include administrative offices and the current library), a service building/print shop, a gym and cafeteria building, and a women's residence hall. Men lived in rooms rented from townspeople, mostly from members of Lincoln Christian Church. Four girls lived in each dormitory room—a small room with four bunk beds, two dressers with drawers, and two small closets. It's a good thing that hardly anyone had many belongings. But by and large, the girls in each room got along well. The faculty was small: some were very competent, some rather mediocre. But all of the faculty cared deeply about students and saw their mission as more than merely presenting material in classes. One of my first tasks was to find a job. A man from my home church had decided to pay my tuition (a huge seventy dollars per semester). I had a small amount of money saved. Mother sent me five dollars every two weeks from the milk check because one of my Jersey cows produced a significant part of the milk sold to the local cheese factory. But I had to find a way to make some money.

I found a job at Lord's Dress Shop, a small retail store for women's apparel downtown on the square. I usually worked Friday and Saturday except for the Christmas season when I often worked every afternoon. Those fourteen hours a week during the "normal" week brought in about $10 a week, before taxes, enough to pay for my room and board at the school, with enough left over to eat two meals each week in a restaurant downtown and to take a taxi back to campus when I got off work on Friday night. (Female students were not allowed to walk to and from campus after dark, requiring that we take a taxi unless we could arrange a ride with someone else who worked the same hours we did.) I never had any money to go to a movie or do anything for recreation, but neither was I ever in need. I always had enough.

Students at Lincoln who weren't preaching or otherwise employed by a church were divided into gospel teams, about ten people to a team. These teams went to churches on Sunday morning (sometimes they left on Saturday evening) where they sang, preached, taught Sunday School, and led youth groups. Many students went to great length to avoid going, but I always enjoyed going and gained valuable experience in teaching and leading. I went on a gospel team at least a couple of times a month during my freshman and sophomore years. Most of the remainder of the weekends I spent in Lincoln and attended Lincoln Christian Church. These were good experiences for me—a time of discovery—as I learned that I could teach effectively. And the opportunities to stay in homes taught me how to be gracious and appreciative of the hospitality extended to us.

Finally, when I was a junior and senior, I graded papers for the English professor instead of working downtown. A job on campus allowed me to go home more frequently. During my junior year I had a ride home every week with a couple who preached across the county. It saved money for laundry and weekend meals if I went home, and I was also able to teach youth in my home church. Since my family always had its own meat in the freezer, my mother gave the couple with whom I rode a package of meat as payment.

I had little time for recreation. My time was tightly regulated with study, classes, work, and weekend ministry. But college was a good time for me. I did well in my studies, developed independence, made good friends who have lasted a lifetime, and learned the skills of teaching and leading.

One extra-curricular activity that I made time to attend was World Evangelism Fellowship. Once or twice a month a missionary visited campus and spoke. That was priceless! I heard people such as Gertrude Morse, Charles and Roberta Selby, Mark Maxey, and Isabel Dittemore present their stories and the work they were doing. All of the speakers gave amazing insights into cross cultural missions and provided illustrations of what God was doing in the world.

The fall of my senior year brought a new opportunity. I was contacted by an elder at First Christian Church in Tuscola, Illinois, asking if I would be interested in a youth ministry there. They had never had a youth minister, but the church was growing and they now needed one. They hoped to start a church kindergarten in the fall and would combine that job with the part-time youth ministry to create a full-time job. I was, of course, interested: this is what I had gone to school to prepare to do. In late September, I rode to Tuscola with a student from that congregation to be interviewed, and I began my work in late October 1961. I was still grading English papers, but I had only twenty-one required hours to take my senior year. I left Lincoln Friday at noon and rode with the student from the church. I was in Tuscola until Monday afternoon when I rode back to school with the same person. I made twenty-five dollars a week—a tenth went to the student to pay for the ride and five dollars went to the lady with whom I stayed and who provided my meals. The $17.50 left from the Tuscola paycheck plus about $10 per week from the college for grading papers made my financial life much easier.

I continued riding with the student until spring break of my senior year. At that time, I bought my first car—a 1956 Ford. Gasoline was only sixteen to eighteen cents per gallon. That car didn't last very long, unfortunately. By January, after I had graduated from college, repair bills became too much and I was given the opportunity to buy a new Falcon with only sixty-five dollars per month payments, certainly possible with a full-time job. Having my own car allowed me to drive to Tuscola for occasional events during the week and gave me flexibility coming and going each weekend.

I graduated summa cum laude from Lincoln Christian College (the name of the institution had been changed January 1, 1962) on June 1, 1962. And on that same day I carried my application to the seminary to the registrar's office at the encouragement of my Christian education professor, Gerald Fargusson. On June 2, I moved everything to Tuscola and began a full-time ministry.

My job at Tuscola was exactly as it had been envisioned when I was called. I would be half-time youth minister, half-time kindergarten teacher for a new church kindergarten to be opened in September. I spent the summer preparing for kindergarten and immersing myself in youth work.

The youth ministry was slow to develop. When I had been called to be youth minister, I was told that it would have to be built from the ground up. Little did I know! Sunday evening groups for juniors (fourth, fifth, and sixth graders), junior high (seventh and eighth graders), and high school kids were meeting. If we had fifteen or sixteen present on Sunday evening, we had a big evening—and half of them were members of three or four families. The men in most of the families worked at the local chemical plant, many of them on the swing shift. Most families had moved to our community from southern Illinois, which meant that many families went back to southern Illinois for their long weekends. That always put a crimp in the youth group attendance!

Although a number of kids were involved at one time or another in the youth program, especially during the summer activities, youth group attendance didn't inch up much during the first couple of years. Fortunately, the church leaders were patient, and they and the minister were more interested in changes in kids than they were in sheer numbers. By the spring of 1963, nearly two years after my beginning at the church, we turned a corner. Quality volunteer youth leaders had been identified, recruited, and trained. Kids became increasingly consistent in their involvement. By the time I left in 1965, we usually had about seventy kids every Sunday evening. The teenage group was especially active.

I worked with a highly competent and caring minister during my time at Tuscola. Bruce Parmenter was a superb preacher and a strong counselor. The church grew by approximately thirty percent in those four years, and a new building was constructed and occupied, providing additional functional space. As I look back, I can be grateful to Bruce, who later taught at Lincoln Christian College and Friends University and also developed a professional counseling ministry, and church leaders for an affirming first place to minister. People were patient with my mistakes and appreciative of the successes.

I began graduate school in the fall of 1962. It took me three years to complete a 30-hour master's degree—a slow pace. I took four four-hour reading courses in Christian education philosophy, curriculum, history, and leadership. I drove to the seminary one afternoon each week to work on the reading courses or to take a course. I also took four courses in education during summer school at the University of Illinois and transferred those to Lincoln to count on the degree. All of the class work was finished in two years, and I spent the third year working on my thesis.

In the fall of 1964, I was asked to teach as a graduate assistant at Lincoln. The church hired someone else to teach kindergarten, and I continued as youth minister. I followed a schedule much like my senior year in college; that is, in Tuscola from Friday afternoon through Monday afternoon, and in Lincoln the remainder of the week.

I taught two sections of a new course—Introduction to Christian Education—and two sections of Methods and Techniques of Teaching the first semester. I added a section of Vacation Bible School in the spring term. I loved the challenge of teaching—preparation, presentation, interaction with students, everything related to teaching in a small college. And I finished my thesis, graduating in June 1965 with a Master of Arts in Christian Education.

The main drawback to my new arrangement was that I would not be teaching at Lincoln another year and I had no full-time job at Tuscola. But even that didn't turn out to be a major problem, for I was offered a position as Director of Christian Education at the Church of Christ in Buchanan, Michigan, at that time the largest Christian church in the state. I followed a very popular Christian education director who had left to go to Great Lakes Bible College in Lansing to teach.

The educational program was well organized, thanks to the previous Christian education director, but it was governed by rigid policies, no matter if they were functional. Board meetings were usually hassles. The good thing was that I, as a woman, couldn't attend except to make my report after which I left. This was despite the fact that the secretary of the board was a prominent woman in the church who was known to leave out key minutes of previous meetings if she disapproved of the results.

It was not my happiest experience in a church. It was instead extremely frustrating and puzzling to me after having served a healthy church with good leaders and generally affirming attitudes. I had been there about a year when I was contacted about taking a teaching position in a Bible college—and I jumped at the chance. I left there in January 1967 to strike out to the west and even more on my own than I had been.

I was five-and-a-half years into ministry. I had seen both the good and the ugly sides of church leadership. I knew that I loved working in the church, but not in Buchanan. And I knew that I wanted very much to teach. So the earliest chapter of ministry closed, and a new one was ready to begin.

Chapter 3

Go West, Young Lady

In late October 1966, I was contacted by Billy Junkins, the president of Midwest Christian College in Oklahoma City, with an offer of a teaching position in Christian education. I knew little about the college, although I did know the president from his days in ministry in central Illinois. I agreed to go for an interview.

Not much commended Midwest as a prospective employer. The college had been in existence since 1945. But it had always struggled financially, and it was no different in 1966 than it had been in the previous years. When I went for the interview, faculty salaries were in arrears by about six weeks.

The college was located on a spacious campus with lots of trees in northeast Oklahoma City, but the buildings on the campus were inadequate. Offices, classrooms, and library were located in a large house on the grounds. The cafeteria was an old, renovated building, and the music classes were held in another old building. The only newer building on campus was a U-shaped dormitory, one wing serving men, the other women, with an apartment for the supervisor located between.

College enrollment was perhaps sixty-five. The faculty had been depleted for a variety of reasons, and President Junkins was making a concerted effort to hire three new faculty members before the beginning of the second semester. I knew the full-time music professor from college days. I had not met the part-time music professor or the two professors who taught languages, missions, and some Bible classes. I met most of the students who impressed me with their enthusiasm, inquisitive minds, and desire to serve God. I spoke in chapel and was encouraged by the current faculty to join them: they thought they needed a full-time female presence to encourage the women. The decision to take the position was not as irrational as it may have seemed. And it turned out to be one of the best decisions I have ever made.

Back in Buchanan, I resigned and set about finishing my work there. My last Sunday was the second Sunday in January 1967. Loading what I owned (mostly books and clothing) in a small U-Haul trailer, I set out for the west accompanied by my mother.

Mother and I arrived in Oklahoma City on Wednesday before I was to begin teaching on Tuesday the following week. My office belongings were unloaded quickly, and I took Mother to the airport to return to Illinois. Vernon Rodgers, the minister at Draper Park Christian Church, spent a day taking me to various apartment complexes to find a place to live. An affordable furnished one-bedroom apartment was located on S.W. 43 Street, a twenty-minute drive from school. It was available right away, allowing me to move in and get mostly settled before the semester began.

From the beginning I loved Midwest, the students, and the ministry. As I recall, I taught fourteen credit hours the first semester. Very soon I was traveling many weekends to do teacher development seminars in churches in Kansas and Oklahoma. I attended the Draper Park Christian Church and quickly was welcomed into the lives of the people.

Draper Park had many special families. One was Jim and Mildred Murray. They had a son who was a junior at the college, a daughter who was a freshman at Oklahoma University, and another son, about twenty-two, who had cerebral palsy and lived at home with his parents. I ate Sunday dinner with them almost every Sunday when I was at home during the first semester I was in Oklahoma City. Others who made me feel accepted and very much a part of the church were Forest and Betha Hines, Lee and Fannie Ransom, Harold and Eugenia Short, Mildred Carroll, Margie Chandler, and Bonnie McKinzie, still my good friend nearly fifty years later. Going west had expanded my world and provided an extended family that continues to this day with those who are still living.

One of my first weekends away from Oklahoma City was a flight with Howard Davis on his small airplane to go to a fifth Sunday rally in Copeland, Kansas. We flew to Copeland and landed in a field just outside town. A large crowd awaited us, which did seem a bit strange, but we were glad to see that we had a ride into town. When we got off the plane, we found that the crowd was awaiting the arrival of Miss Kansas who was to visit the area that day. Can you imagine how disappointed they were?

I went back to Illinois in April for my brother-in-law's ordination to ministry. And I shared with him the name of a church in Enid, Oklahoma that was looking for an associate minister to lead Christian education. Gary was called to that position, and he and Jean moved to Oklahoma as soon as he graduated from Lincoln Christian College. It was especially good to have them only ninety miles away.

Unfortunately, their ministry in Oklahoma was very short—only a year in length. It started well enough, and they were able to adopt a baby about six months after they arrived. They wanted a child very much, and he knew that he could not father a child. It was a time of great rejoicing.

Rejoicing turned to mourning all too soon. A couple of months after they got the little girl, Gary experienced severe kidney and intestinal problems that required surgery to empty waste into a bag outside the body. He had the surgery at University Hospital in Oklahoma City—a surgery that required several hours followed by an emergency surgery again a few hours later. It was touch and go for a time though he recovered enough to go home. Mother had come to help for a couple of weeks, so my sister, the baby, Mother, and I lived in my one-bedroom 700-square foot apartment.

Gary went home, but he didn't fully recover. He was never able to go back to work full time. In June, he was diagnosed with liver cancer for which there was no treatment at that time. A looming concern for him and the whole family was the completion of the adoption of the baby. My parents went to the court in Garfield County, Oklahoma and assured the judge that they would guarantee that the child would be adequately supported if my sister needed the help. He agreed and finalized the adoption the day before Gary died. Gary was very much aware and passed away peacefully in July. He was but 30 years old.

Gary's death was something of a spiritual crisis for me and for all the family. He had lived a life far from the Lord in his late teens and early twenties. Then he had turned to the Lord and prepared for ministry. He pursued his Christian life and ministry with zeal. So why would God allow his life to be snuffed out so prematurely? It is an unanswerable question, of course, but I had to work through it to affirm that God is loving and good and permits what is best for us and to achieve His purposes. It was for me an exercise in trusting God and of affirming what I had been taught and believed intellectually about God. Letting emotions catch up with intellect brought me closer to God and more committed to Him.

A major event on the Midwest campus each fall was the Midwest Christian Convention, which met at a large auditorium a short distance from campus. The convention featured preaching, workshops, music, and usually showcased various groups from the college.

During the summer, all faculty members were expected to attend one or more camps to promote the college among high school students. That first summer I was assigned in early June to a camp that met in rented facilities at a state park near Muskogee and to a week at King Solomon Christian Camp near Abilene, Kansas in August. In between I attended summer school at the University of Illinois for eight weeks, beginning work on an Ed.M. in educational psychology. These two camps were mine to attend for the next four years. And I finished the degree at Illinois in 1969.

The 1967-68 school years found me taking on a new challenge. Vernon Rodgers asked me to serve part-time as Director of Christian Education at Draper Park Christian Church. It was a short two-year ministry, but one that established a foundation for youth ministry at the church.

I performed the various tasks of a Christian education director, but I spent much of my time with high school kids developing a youth program. We had some fine young people in the group, and I had what I considered a good ministry with them.

It is interesting in retrospect. In every possible way, I served as a youth minister and did other ministerial work. But if you were to look today at a list of ministers who have served Draper Park, my name wouldn't be among them. It would be noted that I once led the Bible School program!

Faculty at MCC always taught heavy loads. I was no exception. Sometimes faculty had to teach outside their academic expertise. I was no exception to that either. I taught Speech a couple of years, English one year, and Pastoral Counseling one year. Each was a challenge, but the job was accomplished.

I took on other responsibilities at the college as well. The school very much needed some way to get students into churches to gain experience in teaching. I was assigned the responsibility to develop a program. I worked with the music professor, and we developed two teams—a music team and a drama team, each with about ten students. Each team traveled twice a month on the average, the music professor with the musical group and I with the drama team. We visited many churches in Oklahoma and Kansas, some in Texas, New Mexico, and Colorado. This provided students with practical experience, especially since a visit usually required students to teach classes and lead youth groups as well as the music or drama presentation. It gave MCC a presence in and service to the churches. Each church was asked to fill out an evaluation form to provide feedback that could help the students improve.

When I wasn't traveling with a group, I conducted teacher development workshops in churches about once a month. It made for a busy life, but I was young and physically able and enjoyed it all very much.

Another responsibility I was given was to administer small loans to students who needed $100 or less for short-term emergencies. Someone had given the school money for such a purpose. To be sure the funds didn't disappear to meet a need in the general fund, the loan fund was set up with a separate bank account controlled only by the administrator of the fund who made monthly reports to the President. This fund was a lifesaver to many students, especially some of the married students who sometimes ran short of money to buy groceries for their families until they were paid at the churches where they served. Though it was another responsibility, it didn't require much time and it was a pleasure to see students relieved from undue stress. They were faithful in repaying the loans: no loan was ever in default.

Midway in my four-and-a-half years at MCC, I began to realize that if I were to continue teaching, I needed to get more education. Another factor entered into my thinking. The President of the college, a faculty member who had succeeded Mr. Junkins, was becoming increasingly erratic and autocratic in his leadership. It seemed likely to me that I could be in a position where I needed to seek another ministry. Further education would strengthen my credentials to pursue another place of service.

My first effort was to apply to enter an Ed.D. program at Oklahoma State University. Stillwater was but sixty miles from campus, and I could drive there to take classes one afternoon and evening per week. I was admitted to the program and took two classes—five credit hours. I didn't find this program wholly satisfactory, however, with classes not presenting much challenge, certainly not what I had been accustomed to at Illinois. I decided to wait on doing a doctoral program until I could enter a program better suited to me.

Meanwhile, it became clear that I needed to consider leaving MCC. I was at a church in western Oklahoma one Sunday evening when the minister, a good friend, asked to speak to me privately. He asked why I was leaving MCC. I told him that I hadn't yet decided what I was going to do. He then told me that the President was taking applications for my position. He knew this because one of those contacted was a good friend of his who had called him for an assessment of the situation at the college. Clearly, I had to begin making plans to leave, perhaps as early as that fall.

I confronted the President the next day. He, of course, could make no believable explanation. We worked it out that I would teach at least another year. But I set to work to make the decision of where to pursue doctoral studies, deciding that this would be the logical next step.

I spent the next school year adding a few more courses to my resume by enrolling at Central (OK) State University in Edmond, only twenty minutes from the MCC campus. I took courses that would help me toward a teaching license in Illinois should I need to do that to find work. I applied for the doctoral program in educational psychology at the University of Illinois to which I was accepted with assignment to the adviser I had requested.

Meanwhile, the church at Tuscola, Illinois was looking for a staff member to lead the education program. They could afford to support someone about three-quarters time, which worked perfectly for me to work and go to school. Soon I was wrapping up my responsibilities at the college and preparing to return to Illinois in June.

These years in Oklahoma City were in some ways very difficult. We were always a week or so behind in salaries, a somewhat anxiety-producing situation though it probably taught me lessons that have lasted a lifetime about living frugally and paying some bills a month ahead of time as I could to avoid undue stress if I didn't have the money at the moment the bill came due. Top administrative leadership was weak and largely ineffective, trying to compensate by creating fear and controlling every move of those he was supposed to lead, in the end resulting in insecurity and resentment among faculty.

But for all the difficulties I can cite far more positive experiences: discovering that I could teach effectively, finding talents and interests that were developed when I took on added responsibilities, becoming part of a loving church family that differed significantly from the unhealthy church climate in Michigan, preparing students, many of whom have served faithfully in the church through the years, making friendships that have lasted for almost fifty years, settling on a field of study for my doctoral program, and making friends for myself and for the school among the churches where I traveled often. These rewards far outweighed the difficult times. It was then bitter sweet to leave. I loved MCC and what I was doing and would have preferred not to leave. But I looked forward to returning to Tuscola where I had already established friendships and respect and to going to school at a respected university with a challenging program.

Chapter 4

A Busy Interim

I arrived in Illinois eager to begin both my ministry and school. I arrived the early part of June 1971, and immediately enrolled in one summer school class and began work with youth. It made for a busy summer.

In the fall I took two classes at the university, one that provided insights that forever changed my teaching. It was a course from the Psychology Department—we had to take two courses outside our department. It was Attitude Theory and examined the research dealing with attitude change and strategies to facilitate change. I discovered that attitudes tend to change when people are in caring groups that demonstrate belief as well as hearing it. Before that I had looked at teaching as largely presenting material and making some application of it. Now I began to see that the setting for teaching and the environment in which it is done is as critical as the information. The person who feels at home in a group finds support to raise questions, to practice biblical truth in life, and to live a life to glorify God.

It provided a framework for my own practice of teaching and how I taught others to teach.

I took classes for two summers as well as the two semesters of each of two school years. At the church I kept very busy as well.

A crisis loomed early in the second semester of my first year. The minister, an able man and a good preacher, went off on a tangent, deciding that the institutional church is a sinful idea and that a paid ministry is wrong. It was a widespread teaching during that era. He had bought into the idea. He resigned his position, found a job, and left the church—and convinced thirty others to leave the church. From one Sunday to the next I lost eight Sunday School teachers—a hefty number in a Sunday School of two hundred! And the church was left without a preacher.

The elders wisely decided to take some time—it turned out to be about a year—to find a new minister. They worked with Lincoln Christian College faculty to fill the pulpit, much of the time by a beloved former pastor who taught at LCC. But that meant that I had to assume some of the day-to-day responsibilities of a minster—hospital calling, following up with visitors, and meeting other pastoral needs. That created enough stress, but in addition it appeared that the church might not be able to afford my position. That raised the stress level a few more bars. I thought I had followed the Spirit's leading to re-locate and go to school. Now it appeared that I might not be able to finish, at least not without incurring a large debt. As it was, I was accumulating some debt—and it didn't seem prudent to add any more.

I decided to apply for a graduate teaching assistantship at the university for the next year. It would pay tuition and about four hundred dollars per month. That would be a big help. I applied—and got it. That was but one more affirmation of God's provision. When it became apparent that the church would be able to keep me for the next year, the elders kindly encouraged me to take the assistantship. It was a generous gesture on their part, a kindness I've never forgotten. I am deeply indebted to that church for giving me my first chance at ministry and for their generosity to allow me to finish the doctoral classwork.

A life-shaping event occurred a few months after the minister left. Two women came to me one day and asked me to be a part of a small group. They explained that they and their husbands had decided to form a small Bible study group where they could support each other and pray and study together. Both couples were leaders in the church and both had been close to the previous minister. They felt the need to meet together for study and as a means of refocusing on their Christian lives, to mull over all that had happened in the last few months, and to pray for the church. I needed the group more than they did, they believed, because of the heavy load I was carrying. Furthermore, they asserted, they did not want me to be the leader of the group—their husbands would take turns doing that. I didn't need another thing to do, they believed.

It was a magnanimous gift, providing exactly what I needed. I have to think that they were prompted by the Spirit, another of God's provisions at the right moment. They became family to me, encouraging when I sometimes became overwhelmed, motivating when energy waned, and extending uncommon friendship. I'm not at all certain that I would have stayed the course had it not been for them. These friendships have lasted for all these years.

All too soon, my two years of classwork were drawing to a close. It was time to take written comprehensive examinations. I wrote the examinations in April. I had prepared thoroughly for them. I began the first of the semester to set up a reading program that got me up at 5:30 a.m., followed by reading for two hours before eating breakfast and going to work wherever I was supposed to be that day—the university or the church. The regimen paid dividends, however, for I passed the examinations strongly.

I had intended to stay at Tuscola until my dissertation was finished, after which I expected to pursue a teaching position. The crisis at the church made that desire questionable. So when the Lincoln (Illinois) Christian Church contacted me in the late winter of my second year at the university, I gave it serious consideration. I would like to think that with the guidance of the Lord, I would profit immensely from practical experience in a large church. Up to this time, my work had been in churches of 200-400. But the Lincoln church averaged about seven hundred fifty for worship. I would learn important lessons—and I thought I had something to contribute to them.

It took some time to negotiate the arrangements at Lincoln. I was unwilling to suspend taking my oral examinations or working on the dissertation the following year. I had known far too many people who finished all their coursework but never finished the dissertation, and I did not want to be in that number, given my desire to teach. We agreed that I could choose a day a week to go to the university to do research and writing. I had asked if it would be possible for me to teach at LCC, if asked, and we agreed that I should wait a year while I was finishing the degree, but that I could do so the following year. Financial terms were laid out—and I was to begin work July 1.

I finished the course I was taking, the examinations at the university, and wrapped up my work at the church. My last major activity at the church was Vacation Bible School. I disliked parting again with good friends who had been generous and personally helpful as well as strong partners in ministry. But I looked forward to new challenges and personal growth.

Those two years back in Tuscola could never be described as easy. They were hard in many ways. But they were good years. I learned—again—that I could do what I didn't think I could. I learned that I could teach and relate to university students as well as I had taught Bible college students and that many university students were elated to find a Christian instructor. And above all, I again found God faithful. Not a bad two years!

Chapter 5

LINCOLN: NEW CHALLENGES, NEW OPPORTUNITIES

Late June 1973, found me on the road to Lincoln, following my brother's truck through a rain shower. Fortunately, nothing was damaged and we moved my office content into the office I was assigned at the church and my furniture and personal materials into my two-bedroom apartment in east Lincoln.

Lincoln Christian Church

The Lincoln Christian Church was an old historic church that had met in facilities near downtown Lincoln for a century or so. It was at the time the largest Christian Church in the State of Illinois. The church had demonstrated extraordinary vision by establishing what was then known as Lincoln Bible Institute in 1944. For a few years college classes were conducted in a building near the church and at the church building. For even more years the college didn't have a residence hall for men, and for the most part they rented rooms from various church families. The first President of the college was also the pastor of the church, a position he filled for seven years before assuming the presidency full-time.

His successor had led the church into strong numerical growth with attendance reaching a thousand to twelve hundred before another church had been planted in Lincoln. Equally important, the church continued to demonstrate visionary leadership, this time leading in the establishment of a Christian nursing home in Lincoln. Area churches participated in the project, but the Lincoln church provided the office space and leadership to get the job done. In rapid order additional homes were established throughout Illinois; finally even in Missouri, Iowa, and Indiana, all under the corporate name Christian Homes, Inc.

The church was one of only a handful to have a Bible class and activities for special-needs learners. The class had been started a few years before to meet the needs of two families in the church who had children with profound needs. Those children had since moved away or been institutionalized, but the ministry continued, becoming a ministry to and with developmentally deficient adults. Many of the adults had once lived in the state facility for the mentally handicapped in Lincoln, but the state had initiated a new policy of placing the ablest of these adults in halfway houses, where they lived in congregate arrangements and held menial jobs in the community. This turned out to be a strong ministry, thanks to the able leadership of Ann Myers who was trained in special education and was masterful at dealing with these adults.

By the time I arrived in Lincoln, the church was still strong and engaged with the college, Christian Homes, and a variety of other visionary and outreach efforts. I was the first woman to serve on the pastoral staff of the church, visionary in and of itself, as far as Christian churches were concerned. I never felt much prejudice about a woman in ministry. A bit of concern was expressed early. But I had been there only a month when the senior minister left and only about four months when the youth minister, who had been there for many years, was incapacitated as a result of back surgery. The congregants found out that I could do hospital calling as well as the men had, and what concern there was about a woman on the staff faded quickly.

But the church had some internal issues, especially among the elders and deacons, that needed attention. The problems didn't inhibit ministry, but they did create underlying tensions much of the time. Now and then, the tensions erupted into a bigger issue. This tension would rear its head in unexpected ways occasionally, requiring all staff members to direct attention that direction.

The First Year

I had the challenge to fill over a hundred volunteer positions every week to staff Sunday School and graded worship programs. That meant that about one of every six members had to be involved on a weekly basis with my areas of ministry alone, not to speak of youth and music programs. That first year was a particularly large challenge, for some areas had been seriously neglected in finding and training good volunteers and in supervising curriculum. Those two activities consumed most of my time the first year.

Even so, the Christian Education Committee and I found time to think creatively about what we could do to reach out into the community. We explored the idea of a preschool program for three- and four-year-old children and found a large need existed in the city and immediate area. We set out to work toward state licensure and to find a qualified teacher, with the goal of beginning the preschool in September 1974. Our mission was to provide the highest quality preschool experience we could to give children the best start they could have in life.

The licensure process was tedious and sometimes annoying, but we finished it. We hired an excellent preschool teacher from the public schools who would teach three-year-olds on Tuesday and Thursday and four-year-olds on Monday, Wednesday, and Friday. We also hired an aide for the teacher, a woman who proved priceless. The school opened in September 1974, as scheduled, with twenty four-year-olds and eighteen three-year-olds enrolled. (This was capacity.) The next year we added an afternoon class for four-year-olds—and again were at capacity. The following year we added an afternoon class for three-year-olds—and again were at capacity. By this time we were serving nearly eighty preschoolers each week. The teachers (there were two when we added the afternoon classes) were required to make at least two home visits to every child, a practice that paid large dividends. By the second visit, parents asked a variety of questions about childrearing and spiritual teaching of young children. Several of those families began to attend our church because of these contacts and because we could assure parents that the teaching on Sunday was also high quality. The preschool continues to this day.

The youth program at the church had languished for a few years. With the coming of a new senior minister in 1974, he began to strategize to move the current youth minister into a new position and call a younger, more vibrant youth minister. He succeeded but not without some ruffled feathers and resistance on the part of the current youth minister. It created a certain amount of friction, but the change was made. And a stellar youth program was the result of the work of the new youth minister. It was common for us to have about seventy high school kids involved in Sunday School and again on Sunday evening. He developed some outstanding volunteers—using the ICL training program, explained below, to help in their development. This group was involved in a wide variety of service activities. Students left high school knowing how to serve and being grounded in Scripture, several of them becoming ministers and missionaries, others leaders in the community and church. Each summer I led a camp for fourth grade children at the area camp, and I recruited many of these young people to work with the children in camp. They never disappointed me!

Recruitment and Training of Volunteers

A never-ending task was recruitment and training of volunteers. Recruitment is quite simply work. But we began to develop a two-faceted means to address the issue. One of the chief excuses would-be volunteers cite is, "I don't know enough to teach the Bible to others." To solve the problem for the long term, we decided to enroll in the Bethel Series, a systematic study program designed to develop biblical literacy. It wouldn't solve the problem overnight, but it would lay a foundation for the future. To alleviate the woeful ignorance of the Bible in his congregation, the Bethel Series had been developed by a Lutheran pastor twenty years before. It required a high level of commitment. Teaching methods included picture concepts—a new picture each week—, memorization of key biblical concepts and where to find them, discussion and lecture as well as reading the biblical text each week. It is an outstanding program that met with initial success in the congregation.

The second aspect of training volunteers dealt with how to teach. Some people turned down the invitation to share in the teaching ministry simply because they had no idea of how to develop or present a lesson. We did a lot of training within the congregation, of course. But the International Center for Learning, a part of Gospel Light Publications, conducted quality workshops at churches who hosted them and area churches for teaching workshops that began on Thursday evening, met all day Friday, and lasted until noon on Saturday. This was altogether about twelve hours of training geared to a specific age group. We spent a significant amount of time convincing the ICL leaders that though Lincoln was not a metropolitan area, it was at the center of a large population area and that we were a church with widespread influence. They agreed to come in the spring of 1975—we hosted three workshops if I remember correctly. We paid the fees for our teachers and over the years had approximately seventy per cent of our volunteers involved. It improved the quality of our Sunday School and helped us make some overdue changes In how we conducted our ministry.

Finishing the Ph.D.

During the first year I was in Lincoln, I was working on my dissertation, finishing the first draft by the time the 1974-75 school term began. I began teaching a couple of courses at LCC that fall, finding it gratifying and a way to extend the church's ministry to the campus. The dissertation was completed, defended, and deposited at the university by the first of November, three-and-a-half years after the program had begun. I was delighted to be finished with that phase of life! Now I could turn to other interests and needs.

I have often commented about the response once the Ph.D. was completed. I didn't know one more thing the day after the degree was finished than I did the day before, but one would never have believed it given the response of people far and wide. I had any number of interesting job offers, but I was not ready to consider any of them seriously. I looked into only one and decided it wasn't for me. I continued my work at the church and teaching at the college until 1976. At that time I was invited to join the faculty at Lincoln on a full-tine basis. That invitation I was compelled to consider, for I had always hoped to teach at LCC. So my roles reversed. The church re-organized the staff, and I became the children's minister, responsible for all parts of the teaching program for birth through grade 4. I did that part-time while teaching at LCC full-time. Not much changed except for the number of hours I spent at each place. I was at the church almost every day, and volunteers were welcome to contact me at the college as they needed me. That arrangement worked very well.

Enjoying a reception in my honor upon finishing the Ph.D.

Introduction to Emmanuel School of Religion

In the summer of 1975, I began what turned out to be a 33-year association with Emmanuel School of Religion (now Emmanuel Christian Seminary) when I accepted an invitation to teach a two-week summer class. I missed only one summer in the next twenty as I taught three courses in sequence over a three-year period—Ministry to Children, Ministry to Youth, and Ministry to Adults. It was always a highlight of the year, and I made many new friends in Tennessee. When I moved there in 1994, it was quite an easy transition.

Gaining a World Perspective

I had always been interested in cross-cultural missionary work. I had a friend who was a nurse at Kulpahar Kids' Home in Uttar Pradesh in central India. She wanted me to visit—she harbored a hope that I would agree to go to India to head up the school at the mission. This was a mission for which I had high respect, so I decided to go in late December/early January 1976-77. It was a life-changing trip for me.

A friend and I left St. Louis on Christmas Eve to fly to New York to board Pan Am's round-the-world flight that would land in Delhi the morning of December 26. It was my first trip outside the United States, heightening the fascination as we had short stays in airports in London, Frankfort, and Tehran. And then it was India—so different than either the United States or Europe. My friend was there to greet us and to help us through the challenge of changing dollars to rupees, finding transportation to a hotel, and changing our flight plans for the next morning to make the rest of the journey. (Our flight had been late and we had missed the flight we were to have taken on to Khajaraho.)

My memories from the first day remind me that every sense was challenged. First it was the smell and the haze over Delhi as we left the airport. It was the result of burning cow dung for heating and cooking. We saw beggar kids in the streets. Predictably, we saw a snake charmer alongside the road. People pressed in from every side. We stayed in a colonial-style hotel from the British era. We visited a noisy, glitzy holiday street bazaar and saw many more beggar kids.

On December 27, we took the last legs of the trip to Khajuraho by plane and to Kulpahar in an ambulance (the largest conveyance available to the mission), which was definitely needed for four adults and all the luggage. There we were exuberantly greeted, complete with flower garlands placed around our necks, by the 180 children who resided at the home. They were a happy contrast to the hollow-eyed, malnourished children we had seen as we passed through villages on the way to Kulpahar. And so began our nearly two-week stay.

Kulpahar Christian Mission had a long history. It had been established a few decades before by the Disciples of Christ, then abandoned. Missionaries from the Christian churches/churches of Christ bought the mission property and began work. However, Kulpahar was in such a remote region that it was nearly impossible to recruit missionary families to make a long-term commitment to the work, in large part because of the difficulty of educating their children who would have to go long distances away to boarding school. However, immediately after World War II, two single women, Leah Moshier and Dolly Chitwood sailed to India intent on a lifetime of service there. They remembered having gone into a number of bombed out cities in Europe on the trip to their chosen place of service. It was before Indian independence. They made contact with the few missionaries remaining at Kulpahar. Settling there, they took in an orphan, then another, followed by others—and Kulpahar Kids Home became a reality. Operating an orphanage called for opening a school that by this time was the premier school in the region, with many Hindu families paying tuition for their children to study there. They did not care that the children were required to take Bible classes as well as the usual academic program. Leah and Dolly had already been at Kulpahar for about thirty years when we visited, and they served many more years. Both died in India and are buried at the mission which continues to serve the region, largely now as a boarding school.

It became advantageous to recruit a nurse to operate the dispensary that cared for the children's needs. My friend Madonna Burget (now Spratt) had responded. She was also a midwife, so the medical work had expanded and reached far into the community and surrounding villages. After we were there, a hospital was built, expanding again the outreach into the community.

We had a captivating stay at Kulpahar. We played with kids who loved the attention and quickly made their way into my heart. We went to school. We observed the work at the dispensary. We visited old forts and other remote villages, some larger than Kulpahar. We watched little Hindu girls herd the cows outside the village each morning and come home again each evening, never once expecting to go to school. We attended church on Sunday morning and evening. We played games with the kids. We went to small teas hosted by staff members for us. We enjoyed the New Year's Day game competition among the school children. We prayed and conversed and studied Scripture with the missionaries. No wonder that this mysterious land of India had crept into my heart to stay!

Too soon it was time to go home—a different person than when I arrived. Dolly and one of the older girls accompanied us on our return to Delhi to catch our flight home. We went first to Agra where we visited the Taj Mahal, one of the seven wonders of the ancient world. It is a large palace built by an ancient Moghul king in 1563 as the place of rest for his beloved wife. The structure is huge and ornate. Words can hardly describe its grandeur. We went from there to Delhi where we took in a sight and sound show the evening before our flight home.

Pramodini, the child from Kulpahar that I sponsored for ten years

The flight home had its own excitement. We had what airline personnel first thought was a fire in the baggage hold in Frankfurt and had to deplane, overnight it turned out. It wasn't a fire, but the hold was filled with smoke because someone had checked through a mattress that had a cigarette smoldering in it. It had activated all the fire extinguishers, and new ones had to be flown in from London. We were taken to the Intercontinental Hotel in Frankfurt where we got about five hours of sleep. Our room was very cold. I was grateful for the German down comforters that kept me warm. We finally arrived back in St. Louis late on a Saturday night, a day late. But what a trip! I had become aware of a much wider world and the desperate poverty of many, both economically and spiritually. It was a few years before I could make much of a contribution to world missions except, of course, in prayers and monetary support, but the day would come a little over two decades later when I could return to India to teach.

Back to Oklahoma City

Back in Lincoln, ministry at the church continued to go well. But the college turned out to be a difficult place for me to serve. The chairman of the Christian education department was long past his prime. He had little if any vision for the future. That was frustrating enough. But beyond that, a considerable amount of friction, mostly between the President and the rest of the personnel, was exceedingly uncomfortable. It seemed that no one trusted anyone. It simply wasn't for me a place that encouraged creativity, energy, or satisfaction. And I sensed a deep unease by many with a woman in a key faculty position, something I had not felt to any degree at the church. It left me pondering the future.

At the same time, Midwest Christian College was looking for a Christian education professor, and they offered me the job. In some ways the move made no sense. Midwest was still small and struggling. It almost certainly would not survive for many more years. But it was a place where I was respected and wanted. I had some deep roots there and in the churches of the city. It would take me from one set of problems to another, but the new set would be among congenial people. I decided to take the position, even if it should be a short-term solution.

I left Lincoln deeply grateful for all the opportunities I had, especially at the church. I was satisfied that I had given all that I could to the situation and that God had blessed those efforts. I was disappointed that the college situation hadn't worked out better. But all in all, my Lincoln years had been good years, and I could move on to new challenges.

Chapter 6

A Brief Sojourn in Oklahoma City

I arrived in Oklahoma City in the summer of 1978, not at all certain what the future would hold. But I was at a healthy church where I was nurtured and valued. And I would be teaching bright, committed young people. For now that was enough.

Developing Writing Skills

I had an extra project as well. Standard Publishing Company had decided to publish a series of textbooks that could be used for biblical and pastoral courses in most Bible colleges. I had been invited, with Charles Gresham and John Wade, professors at Kentucky Christian College and Atlanta Christian College respectively, to publish a book that would be suitable for introductory Christian education classes. I was to serve as the senior editor, managing the details of the project and assuming responsibility for deadlines and other discussions with the editor. I had done some previous work for Standard, mostly writing curriculum for Vacation Bible School, giving me a good working knowledge of the company. It was an opportunity to develop in still another professional area.

The book project required a generous portion of my time. But for once, I was working at only one job, giving me the time I needed. It required a certain level of skill to define what needed to be done by a writer, to read what had been submitted and critique it, and to follow up with demands for better work in one or two cases. In one case, I simply had to reject the submission and send it on to another writer. And, of course, I was to write some chapters myself. Overall, the project went very well and according to schedule. It was a proud moment when I held a copy in my hand. The book turned out to sell well and was reprinted. A few years later I revised it, again using contributing writers.

About the time that book was wrapped up, I was invited to write one in the College Press series, "What the Bible Says About. . ." Mine was to be *What The Bible Says About Sexual Identity.* It was a two-year project from start to finish, most of it finished while I was in Oklahoma City, though the printed book didn't make it off the press until after I had left Midwest.

These writing projects were the interim challenge I needed as I taught at Midwest. Teaching went very well, and I enjoyed my three years back at Midwest. I also spent considerable time in churches conducting workshops on weekends.

The Christian Educator's Conference

The Christian Educators' Conference had for a time met on Monday afternoon through Tuesday noon immediately prior to the opening of the North American Christian Convention. It was a gathering of administrators and faculty from the colleges who met to consider a theme of interest and relevance. It was supervised by a continuation committee composed of elected members from among the schools. The committee planned and publicized the program. Each school paid a small annual fee to provide funds for speakers, hospitality, and publicity. I was asked to be the chair for 1979, a job I did for the next fifteen years until the conference was discontinued. Over the years, schools had been less and less likely to fund faculty members to attend the North American Christian Convention, turning the conference into largely a gathering of presidents. They had other venues for interaction during the year. Gatherings of Bible professors had been promoted at other times to focus on their issues, making it unlikely for them to attend the conference. The responsible action was to cease the conference: it had served its purpose well and now other groups had emerged to better serve those same purposes in specific disciplines and positions. 1993 was the final year for the conference.

A Charming Summer in Michigan

In the summer of 1980, I was invited to Bailey, Michigan, to spend two months evaluating the church's Christian education program, making recommendations for the future, and training teachers. Bailey was a hamlet twenty or so miles north of Grand Rapids where I had access to the Calvin College library and could do research for the book on sexual identity. It was a blissful summer: I had enough to do to keep me happy, but I wasn't so busy but that I could take time to walk daily and to do a good deal of spiritual reflection. I made some good friends and went home refreshed.

Taking the Next Step

I enjoyed my teaching at Midwest. We had some students with a promising future in ministry (many of those realized through the years). Though Midwest was not the place for me permanently, it was the right place at the right time, allowing me to hone writing skills, do important work with students, and be among the churches.

It was evident, however, that the days of Midwest were numbered. I was in no hurry to leave, but I was compelled to consider good opportunities as they presented themselves. I had been contacted by Cincinnati Bible College and Seminary toward the end of my first year at Midwest, a position I declined because I had been at Midwest for such a short time.

Then I was invited to present the Seminary Lectureship in the fall of 1980. I had a delightful time on campus. This was obviously a preliminary test, for I was contacted again, more urgently this time, a few weeks later. It was time to examine the possibility.

I first said I couldn't do it—I had a lawsuit from an automobile accident pending. But they were persistent and the lawsuit was settled out of court, leaving no major obstacles to impede such a move.

It was with a heavy heart that I bid farewell to Oklahoma City and Midwest Christian College, both of which had been good to me. But it was with expectation that I looked forward to where I felt the strong direction of the Spirit to new areas of growth and ministry.

Chapter 7

I Thought Cincinnati Would Be Home Forever

Cincinnati Bible Seminary

I could never have anticipated much of what happened in my Cincinnati tenure. That was undoubtedly good. Otherwise, I might never have been there.

Cincinnati Bible Seminary was one of the three oldest Bible colleges among Restoration churches. It had a colorful background and several revered professors who made the school what it is today. The school was begun in the 1920s, in the era of some of the greatest friction between the Disciples of Christ and the independent Christian churches/churches of Christ. CBS had taken a strongly conservative theological stance led by Professor R. C. Foster and Professor George Mark Elliott. By the time I arrived in 1981, Foster had died. (In fact, his widow died the first weekend I was in Cincinnati). Elliott lived on, however, occupying an office on campus and wielding huge influence on faculty decisions, though he no longer taught any classes. The school had an earlier reputation of being confrontational and combative with those with whom they didn't agree. Much of that had subsided by 1981, though such behavior raised its ugly head now and again, especially during faculty appointments. The college had been particularly conservative in its stance toward what women could and should be and do in the church. Only a few women were on the faculty—two who taught part-time in secretarial studies and two or three who taught in the music department, and me. (The balance changed over the next decade, however.)

The college was led by President Harvey Bream who had been at the helm for at least a decade when I arrived. The academic vice president, who also served as Dean of the college, was a long-time employee—ever since he had finished college about thirty years before. He was only average at best. But the seminary dean was a forward looking, creative man with long pastoral experience.

Enrollment was approximately a thousand, making it one of the larger schools in the American Association of Bible Colleges (now the Association for Biblical Higher Education). The college claimed to have aspirations to achieve regional accreditation with the North Central Association (now the Higher Learning Commission), though little had been done to that end except to hire Dr. Howard Wakefield, a retired University of Wisconsin professor and a CBS graduate, to head up the effort and also to teach a course in the Christian education department. Some preliminary approaches had been made to the North Central, but not much beyond that.

It was a heady time on the campus in 1981. They had made over the previous two years some significant faculty additions with people who were well known among the churches. Enrollment was near its zenith. The school seemed poised to continue its development.

Deciding to Go to Cincinnati

I went to Cincinnati to interview in February 1981. The defined position was a dual appointment as full professor in both the college and seminary and the chairperson for the Department of Christian Education. I decided before I went that I would not take the position if there was even one negative vote from any source—undergraduate faculty, seminary faculty, or trustees—for I reasoned that a negative vote had more to do with gender than with evaluation of professional competence.

The issue of gender came up in the interview with undergraduate professors. One mentioned his concern that I would be supervising men and wanted to know if I would consider the position if I were not chairperson of the department. I responded by saying that I didn't have to be chairperson, but I wanted to be in a position to have significant influence on the future of the department. I wanted to ask him if he would have taken his position if he could not have been chairman of his area, but wisely refrained. The other professors in the Christian education department quickly added that they had no interest in being the chairperson—they wanted someone with academic credentials and ministry experience who could lead the department in the right direction. That dealt with, the vote was unanimous for me to be called.

The interview with seminary professors took quite a different direction. The person whom I would replace had created some embarrassing situations for the college with his theology of the church and its polity. He had condemned existing churches as completely ineffective and non-biblical and proposed that churches that followed his model were the only ones that would thrive and please God. He had been vocal enough that churches were expressing concern and withdrawing support. He had been relieved of a full-time position though he would still teach a course each semester and work with his "model" church that he had planted. The interview probed into my concept of the church and its polity. It went well, and I was given a unanimous invitation to join the faculty.

My final interview was with the trustees. That was basically a pro forma situation, though the trustees were interested in what I might want to lead the department to become. Their vote was also unanimous. I accepted the position and left Oklahoma City in mid-July.

Early Projects

I taught a very heavy load my first year at the college, but I had a graduate assistant, an MCC graduate, who was enrolled in the seminary. He graded papers and helped in a variety of ways. The Christian education curriculum needed serious revision, and that was the first major task I began to work on with my colleagues.

The business education area, which was under my general supervision, also needed revision and begged for a move toward word processing. The instructors were positive about these changes, wanted them very much, but the Dean was resistant. It took more than two school years to get all of those changes made in secretarial studies. But the curriculum revision went smoothly and expeditiously for Christian education.

An interest among the trustees was the development of a program or arrangement that would allow Christian education majors to finish licensure for teaching if they chose that route. That was the top priority item for the department during my second year. The head of the teacher education program at the College of Mount St. Joseph, about five miles from our campus, had at one time been at the University of Cincinnati and had been generous with transfer of credits from CBS to UC. We began to work with him to devise a planned program whereby a student could take a bachelor's degree at CBS and achieve licensure for elementary school teaching at the College of Mount St. Joseph. It turned out to be a five-year program with several of the courses at CMSJ counting toward a master's degree if the student chose. By the end of the third year I was at CBS, we had the program ready for launch. We worked out a similar arrangement for secondary licensure. This work with CMSJ elicited an invitation for me to be on a task force there to evaluate and revise their standards in light of pending new state licensure requirements. The joint program served several students each year.

Standard Publishing Company

I was invited by Standard Publishing Company in 1985 to become a curriculum consultant with the company. My primary job, in addition to the column I was doing for the *Lookout*, was to monitor and evaluate curriculum pieces for Sunday School and Vacation Bible School. It was an assignment I savored and could also use graduate students in various ways. This relationship lasted a decade. By the end of the decade the company decided that they needed to undertake a large curriculum evaluation project, scrutinizing every piece of teaching material they had in preparation for production of a new Sunday School line. I was asked to chair this three-year project that was challenging, sometimes difficult, always satisfying.

Crisis

Life at CBS seemed to be going well—and then the financial roof caved in. It turned out that the school hadn't had an audit in years. The President had made sweetheart financial deals with several faculty. And the coffers were running dry rapidly. The result was that the President was fired and an interim president, who served for two-and-a-half years, brought his considerable financial and management expertise in an attempt to save the school.

Ron Geary was a controversial figure from the first day he stepped on campus. He obviously had to take swift and unpopular action. On the one hand, he put together a fund raising plan that raised a million dollars that summer, keeping the wolf from the door. On the other hand, he was forced to make personnel decisions—and that is where most of the controversy came. He asked two professors beyond retirement age to follow through on retirement. They might teach a course each semester, but at the adjunct rate. He had to reduce another professor, not yet at retirement age, to part-time, but helped him find enough additional teaching at the University of Cincinnati to keep his salary at the same level. A number of part-time instructors were not retained for the following year. Salaries were, of course, frozen for the following year, and contributions to the retirement plan were suspended for a year. None of these moves endeared him to some. Nevertheless, the financial bleeding was stemmed.

His most momentous decision was to go full speed ahead toward regional accreditation. Some on campus argued that no one of right mind would have a faint hope that we could achieve accreditation with the financial crisis. He refused to listen. And because he did, my life changed dramatically.

New Responsibilities

I had been on vacation, but when I returned, the President wanted to see me. His request was that I head up the accreditation effort, pulling together what had already been done, and organizing us to put together a self-study with a goal of a North Central visit in the spring of 1988, a little less than two years hence. I agreed to do it: I was up for a major challenge. And a major challenge it would be, though one I really enjoyed.

A year later he came with an additional request. His analysis of the school indicated that we had an attrition rate that was much too high from freshman to sophomore years. A factor was the still prevailing notion that a year of Bible College was desirable for every student, who could then go on to prepare for a chosen field of study—and for a good many that wasn't at the Bible college. Lack of accreditation was another factor, one that was being addressed diligently. However, much of it seemed to be related to academic advising which needed to be more intense and personal during the freshman year than during subsequent years. This was especially true for students who came from families in which the parents had no college background. President Geary was intent on addressing this problem but was meeting resistance from the Dean. The Dean had a long tenure with the school, and removing him would have created a serious political problem with a half dozen or so influential professors who had been at the school for years. The President's decision, then, was to appoint me Assistant Dean with a specified job—working on the attrition problem—if I would assume the position. Again, it was an interesting challenge, an opportunity to develop expertise in another area. The self-study work had been completed and the first draft written for submission late in the first semester. So I agreed to do it.

We put together a cadre of freshman advisers who were highly relational with students. They were to make three contacts each semester with each advisee. If at the end of the freshman year, a student had focused in on a course of study, such as music or teacher education that would best be served by an adviser from that area, the freshman adviser should facilitate that with me. These advisers were compensated for their extra time and effort as they met certain goals. And the strategy worked. Attrition was reduced by several percentage points the first year and continued to improve from year to year.

Meanwhile, in the midst of all these extra activities, I continued to teach. The number of Christian education majors increased, especially in the seminary where there had been about a half dozen in 1981 when I arrived, to about twenty in 1987-88.

The accreditation effort ended in successful achievement of candidacy status, the obligatory first step before final accreditation. We would have a visit again in two years. Though we would request final accreditation at that time, it wouldn't be unusual for a school to have to spend another two years at the candidate level.

Success meant starting immediately on another self-study. Again the President wanted me to lead that effort.

It wasn't quite as frantic as it had been the first time when I had to dig out what had already been done, then work to fill in the gaps. This time the President, with my input, appointed a committee to carry out the task. The committee appointed subcommittees to gather information, evaluate, and make recommendations for specific areas. The committee met once a month to coordinate the work.

More Change

The trustees named a new president in the fall of 1989. He was a young man with little or no administrative experience. He was by background a speech and debate teacher. He was quite conservative theologically, especially in regard to what women could and should do, leaving me a bit nervous about where this would take us for the future and leaving me open to consideration of offers that might come my way, though I was committed not to seek something else for the time being at least.

My nervousness shot upward after a confrontation one day. He and I were discussing something—I don't remember what—that we agreed on. But he said, "You know, it's too bad God made you a woman." I suppose he meant it as a compliment, but that isn't how I absorbed the statement. I responded, "I don't think God is the problem. I think it lies somewhere else." It was enough for me to listen seriously to a pitch from Central Christian Church in Mesa, Arizona, to join their staff. A number of other off-the-cuff remarks by the new president led me to the conclusion that I would take the position in Arizona. I would finish the school term at Cincinnati, take a four-month mini-sabbatical, and begin in Mesa in October.

I had no more than submitted my resignation than the new president was back in my office, this time full of apologies for his remark and asking me to reconsider my decision. I told him that I would reconsider only if we could go back to the basics and re-negotiate the position entirely. He agreed, and we began work to get the job done.

I told him I was happy doing the self-study work, but that would come to an end in a couple of months, except for follow-up reports, which I would be happy to do. I explained that I no longer wanted to be assistant dean—I had met all the resistance I wanted with the retention project. Now we needed to develop an assessment program to assure that we were meeting educational goals, but the Dean was dragging his feet on this project too. I definitely wanted to teach, and I wanted to be valued as a female faculty member. Remarkably, we worked through all that between ourselves and with the chairman of the trustees. He named me Special Assistant to the President for Academic Development. I taught as usual. I handled accreditation matters and supervised the retention program. Additionally, I was to lead us in the development of an assessment program acceptable to the accreditation agencies and to work out and manage the funds assigned for faculty development. An interesting portfolio! I was assigned a secretary who was invaluable in juggling all the responsibilities. She remained my secretary for as long as I remained at the school.

I actually relished the projects I took on. We developed the assessment program, probably the least effective of the areas for which I was responsible. That was in part because a couple of the academic divisions were slow and somewhat resistant to developing the evaluation tools that would apply to their area. We did get something done—far more than we had ever had before—and it was acceptable to the accreditors at the time, but it could have been much better.

One of the earlier tasks I had was to develop a case for letting an assistant professor go. He was ineffective as a teacher—we had heard enough complaints to know that. When he was employed, he had agreed to pursue the M.Div. degree and move on to doctoral work, but in four years he had taken only one or two courses. His lack of progress in a degree program was well documented. But we had no formal faculty evaluation system beyond a home-made class evaluation form. So his ineffectiveness was more a matter of hearsay than well documented evidence. We did release him, but I vowed to myself that I never wanted to go through another faculty termination without a far better system of producing evidence upon which to base the decision. The President agreed, and development of a systematic evaluation project became part of the faculty development program.

CBS had a cadre of older professors who had been teaching for many years. But with faculty attrition during the financial crisis, a promising group of young faculty members had joined the ranks. None of them had a doctorate, and some of them struggled with one or more aspects of teaching. Our strategy ended up with several elements:

1. A faculty member submitted a plan for the following school year by the first of March. It included courses he or she would teach, what the person would do to improve academically (courses to take, seminars to attend, other experiences that would enhance teaching), and courses he or she would teach that should be evaluated. This allowed these

factors to be figured into the faculty development budget for the next year.
2. In September, the faculty person would meet with the administrator of the program to assess the progress made from the previous year's faculty plan.
3. Full-time faculty members had two courses evaluated by students each semester, one if they were part-time faculty. They could choose at least one of the courses to be evaluated, perhaps both if the administrator agreed. The chosen classes were visited by a faculty member and an administrator who filled out an observation form based on the class session and another form assessing the quality of the course plan distributed to students. At the end of the semester a standard student evaluation form was administered.
4. When the results of class evaluations were tallied, the instructor met with the administrator to go over the results and choose areas of teaching to work to improve.
5. At the time a faculty plan was completed, the data was summarized, with administrative evaluation, and given to the faculty person to see before being filed in the individual's permanent file.

The system worked well (and later at Emmanuel as well). Conversations with instructors led to better teaching, and faculty credentials were vastly improved on the whole. It has always been a source of pride to have been a part of the lives of several who took advanced degrees and some who struggled so seriously in their early years of teaching becoming among the best teachers on the campus.

Beyond Cincinnati

I had continued my interest in missions through the years but only once had visited a mission work. I had done some traveling in Europe and Israel through the 1980s, however. I had become involved with Pioneer Bible Translators as a board member. The organization encouraged one board member each year to visit the work in Papua New Guinea. My turn came in 1984 when I made a journey to that faraway primitive land to work with families who were homeschooling their children. I left Cincinnati on a Monday morning early in July, going first to Atlanta for the Christian Educator's Conference and the opening night of the North American Christian Convention. On Wednesday, I flew to Seattle where I boarded a United flight bound for Hong Kong, a twelve-hour non-stop leg of the journey. I spent a few days in Hong Kong working with personnel from Chinese Christian Mission. (All but one of those involved with the mission had been students at Lincoln Christian Seminary when I taught there; I had been adviser for Wing Wong, one of the team members.)

My first impression of Hong Kong was of the masses of people thronging wherever one went. The city was a mass of high rise apartments and office buildings. Little empty space was left. Public transportation was modern and rapid. Buses were crowded.

On Friday morning two of the missionary families took me out for breakfast. You didn't have to order from a menu. Ladies pushing food carts with various available dishes came by the tables. If she had something you wanted, you stopped her and she gave it to you.

On Saturday evening, one of the families took me to the bazaar. It had all kinds of food stalls and other kiosks with goods to sell. Scattered around the area were several aspiring musical combos, all playing their own tunes. Few of them were very good, and it was the most awful cacophony.

On Sunday I worshiped with one of the churches and in the afternoon conducted a teacher development workshop for volunteers from that church and half dozen others. On Monday night I embarked for Port Moresby in Papua New Guinea.

The Papua New Guinea experience was unlike any I had experienced before. I spent the first week in Madang, the center for the Pioneer Bible Translator work. It was a quaint tropical city—only a few paved streets, one air-conditioned store, and home of most services needed by the missionaries. Contact was made every day via ham radio with those living in the bush. Only one bush station could be reached by land transportation; all the others required a canoe, a Missionary Aviation Fellowship plane to ferry people in and out, or both.

I worked that week with a family who had a first grader. She was not doing as well as she could with her learning progress. She did have a mild case of dyslexia, but more than anything, she could manipulate her mother into a frustrated state that was counterproductive to her progress. We worked on the situation, and I promised to go home and consult with some reading specialists to determine the best approach to overcoming the mild problems she had.

The second week I went to the bush, going to the village of Samban that could be reached only by canoe or airplane. Fortunately, we chose the airplane. There I was with a family with two young boys. The mother was a licensed teacher back in the United States and was doing a superb job with the boys. The older boy, actually a second grader, was reading at eighth grade level. The younger boy, a kindergartener, had some learning problems, but the mother had figured out workable solutions. The boys, of course, didn't like to be in school when their village friends were not. But the mother invited the best friend of each boy to become a student in the school as well—and that solved that problem.

I will never forget my shock when our flight landed on the airstrip outside the village. Out of the forests came many people to greet us—and the women had nothing on from the waist up. During the week in that village, I spent time with the school, observed the translator at work, walked a mile or so to another village to attend a wake, and shared in devotions and prayers with the missionary family. I slept in an Australian mission house located at the far end of the village from the American family. It was necessary for a woman to stay with me—not because I was in any danger, but because it was unacceptable for a single woman to spend a night alone. I usually woke up a time or two in the night hearing rats running around in the rafters! Otherwise, I was in a comfortable place.

The wake deserves description. The missionary couple and I walked close to a mile to a stream that we had to cross. The stream was low in this dry season, but it was very wide. A one-log swinging bridge spanned the chasm—and the log had handrails if you were able to walk about ten feet. It was terrifying! But the missionary told me to hold on to his shoulders and follow him; his wife did the same with the language helper. We made it and continued to walk a short distance to another stream to cross. Our destination was on the other side. Men from the village saw us and came in a canoe to take us across. Then we had to climb up a notched out log to get into the house where we sat cross legged around the body until they took it for burial.

The missionary went to the burial but discouraged his wife and me from going because of the density of mosquitoes at the burial spot. When all was completed, we then made the return trip back to our village.

I was in the village for a week and then flew to another village, somewhat closer to Madang, to spend a week with another family who had children in late middle school and early secondary school. I had a delightful time with this brother and sister. Both were bright and capable, but neither tested well. I discovered that their mother was lenient in allowing them to get up and wander around at their pleasure when they were taking tests or doing seat work. They got their work done, but they had developed some bad habits that would affect them negatively in schools back in the United States. The mother was quick to correct the situation. We also spent time planning their curriculum so they would be prepared for entrance into college when they returned to the States. (The older one would be entering college at the beginning of the family's next furlough.)

Back in Madang, I spent three or four days winding affairs up and drawing up a recommendation for the board regarding a missionary family that had proved troublesome. I flew to Port Moresby and on to Hong Kong where I spent a night in a very nice hotel at the airport. I recall waking up early, ordering breakfast, and watching the Los Angeles Olympics on television as I ate. It was then Hong Kong to Seattle to Cincinnati—and I was home in time to get ready for classes to begin.

I made another trip outside the States in 1988, this time to Mexico for the annual Missionary Reunion. I had been invited to lead the children's program. I took with me three graduate students, and we conducted VBS for the children, complete with the 1988 Standard VBS materials that the company generously provided. We had a wonderful time with two teaching sessions each day with twenty to twenty-five children ages three through twelve. I spent about as much time with missionaries as I did with the children, providing a listening ear and counsel. This was the first of three trips to this reunion—I went again in 1990 and 1992, the last as the main speaker for the adults. On the way home, the students and I spent a half day and a night in Mexico City and were able to take a short guided tour of the city.

Continuing Academic Responsibility

Our next accreditation visit was scheduled for April 1990. We were as ready for it as we could be. And amazingly we were granted full accreditation—not the common practice—at the end of it. Elation filled the campus—and I am grateful that the interim president was still on campus to share firsthand in the celebration. It was a good day for the future of the school. We would next have an accreditation visit in the spring of 1994, the usual North Central practice.

About the time of the accreditation visit, the President appointed me as Dean of the seminary. The able dean who preceded me had become ill and would not return to work on a full-time basis. This action raised a few eyebrows—a woman as dean of the seminary? But the transition was made with little difficulty.

The Sabbatical That Wasn't

I had at one time planned to take advantage of the possibility of a summer and one-semester sabbatical that had been offered to faculty who had been at the school for more than five years. I planned to do cross-cultural work and seek to understand how Christian education is accomplished in those various settings. By late 1988, I had made arrangements with TCM International to spend a summer there. I would make arrangements to spend the fall semester with other missions.

That wasn't to be. When I took the job as Special Assistant to the President in 1989, I forfeited my claim to a sabbatical, for administrators were not eligible for this benefit. I worked it out to go twice to TCM in the summer of 1990, once immediately after the spring term ended and the other in late July. I had a bevy of frequent flyer miles, enough to make both trips and have miles left over, so expense was not a factor.

TCM International had been founded about thirty years previously as Toronto Christian Mission, descriptive of the city where the work initially occurred. Gene Dulin, the founder, was preaching in Toronto and made contact with a number of Russian Christians who put him in touch with Christian leaders in Russia. He began to travel to Russia and other Soviet countries to encourage the Christians. He delivered Bibles, literature, clothing, and financial aid as he could.

Dulin's work soon became the focus of his ministry. He gave up the church where he preached in Toronto and moved to Indianapolis, in a much more accessible location to supporting churches. That prompted a name change—still TCM, but now meaning Taking Christ to the Millions. Eventually the mission purchased a house with a couple of outbuildings about fifteen miles southwest of Vienna near the village of Heiligenkreuz and at the edge of the Vienna Woods.

The house, which became known as Haus Edelweiss, and buildings were a storage place for clothing, Bibles, and literature and a launching point into the eastern European countries where they had contact and ministry. As relations between the United States and the Soviet Union softened, it became possible to bring groups from the various countries once a year to Heiligenkreuz for two-week seminars conducted by visiting professors from America. I would be at two of those conferences in 1990.

The Haus Edelweiss experience opened another new world to me. I met Christians who remained faithful under immense stress. Some had been arrested for their faith; others had been persecuted in other ways. But I found happy, even joyous people who prayed and lived with intensity for the Lord. I came away with a greater understanding of the universal nature of the church and a deep appreciation for those so faithful in such stressful situations.

During my first conference, I taught a couple of hours each day about teaching children. I had fifteen to twenty in the class. They were from Poland, Czech, Estonia, and Belarus. I had three translators—Czech, Estonian, and Russian (for the Polish and Belarussian groups). It was a challenge to develop a cadence that worked with all three languages.

A conference in those days began on Monday evening with a time of orientation for the visitors and a time of prayer for the coming events. We would conduct classes on Tuesday, Wednesday, Thursday, and Friday followed by a day off on Saturday. The visitors and professors were provided transportation to Shopping Center South where they could arrange for free bus transportation on to Vienna to go sightseeing. The Eastern Europeans were provided sack lunches to take with them; the professors usually wanted to visit Figlmüllers, the famous schnitzel restaurant, or Demels, the renowned pastry restaurant, to sample their fares.

Sunday was, of course, a day of worship, a special Sunday dinner, and an afternoon visit to the nearby small city of Baden, there to enjoy a concert in the park. It was back to classes Monday through Thursday with another day off on Friday. We had class on Saturday and shared another Sunday together. Then we had classes Monday through Wednesday. Wednesday evening was a special closing time of thanks and prayer. It was customary in those days for the visitors to give small gifts to the staff and professors as a way of expressing their deep appreciation for what they regarded as the vacation they had never before had. The following morning groups began to depart for home, usually by train.

I became well acquainted with the Czech group who demonstrated exceptional exuberant joy. I forged a friendship with the translator Mila who described to me what it was like to go to Prague the previous Christmas after the wall had fallen. I remember her saying, "It was amazing. I walked through the city square crowded with people—and there were no soldiers with guns!"

I was hooked! I would be back.

I returned in late July as expected. This time we had Hungarians as guests. We followed the same schedule as before, but ended the conference a day earlier because the Hungarians had to leave early. My translator was Suzanne, a Christian Jew from Budapest. Her mother had been incarcerated during World War II, but somehow Suzanne, who was but an infant, was left to the care of her grandmother. Her mother was still living and remembered well the horrors endured by Jews during the war.

These two summer experiences were profound for me—and helped to determine at least a part of my summer through 2005.

By 1991, a new president had ascended at TCM. He traveled through the Eastern European countries to ascertain what TCM could best do for and with them now that they were out from under the yoke of Communism. Distribution of clothing was still important, but the number one priority was training. They believed they could do the ministry—they didn't need missionaries to preach and evangelize—but they needed training to do it. And if they had their preference, they would like academic study that could result in advanced degrees.

Tony Twist, the President of TCM, approached all three seminaries—Emmanuel, Lincoln, and Cincinnati—to see if there would be interest and the possibility of working out some kind of program. Only we at Cincinnati were interested. We worked out a contractual arrangement with TCM to recognize a prescribed course of study that would lead to the Master of Arts in Practical Ministry and another to lead to the Master of Divinity degree. The Dean at Cincinnati would visit annually to observe the program, approve faculty, some of whom might be from Cincinnati, and generally monitor the program to assure academic quality. The contact was in place by 1992, and remained in effect until 2005, when the TCM Institute achieved full accreditation status with the Higher Learning Commission.

I went to Vienna again in 1991, and taught a class at the Haus. Then I joined Bob Shannon, and we flew to Sofia to conduct week-long classes in Bulgaria. These were the first classes, seminars, or even preaching done by TCM in Bulgaria for years. The classes were to be taught at the Holiday House for Miners in the village of Velingrad in southern Bulgaria not far from the Macedonian border. We spent our first night in Bansko with an extended Christian family who treated us generously and graciously. We worshiped in the village where the class met. The church prior to the fall of Communism had been held together by twin sisters who worked tirelessly on behalf of the church. They had done almost all of the teaching and preaching and ministry to the ten or twelve old women in the church. After the fall of Communism, they had intensified their efforts. The day we worshiped with them the attendance was about ninety.

A small group of TCM contacts from Macedonia also attended these classes. We had a lovely evening meal with them alone one evening in a restaurant that was once the Mecca for Communist officials in the area. The Macedonians had jokes galore about Communists. One of them paused at some point in the conversation and said, "Can you believe this? I thought it might never be possible. What changes in the world!"

I returned to TCM in 1992, first teaching a class at the Haus. (Classes were credit classes beginning this year.) From there I went to Hungary where I was met by Laszlo and Mary Gerszenyi, TCM field directors in Hungary, who took me to Balaton Szenec south of Budapest where our class would be conducted.

We arrived in Balaton on Saturday evening. The Gersenyis and I stayed in the home of church members; she the postmistress in the village, he a hydrologist on Lake Balaton. They had comfortable quarters that were rented to tourists during the holiday season late in the summer. We ate breakfast with them—boiled eggs, cucumbers, tomatoes, cheese, yogurt, bread. The house was about two blocks from both the church building and the class site.

The pastor in the village, a wee little man with a huge ministry, had a large youth group that met Saturday evening. The village was teeming with teenagers. On Sunday I preached for the church. The facilities were crammed. He had also asked me to observe all the Sunday School classes. While the children and youth classes met for teaching, the adults gathered in the sanctuary to pray for the church and for the children. Amazingly, I saw a Standard VBS poster carefully preserved in one classroom; it was from VBS materials eight or ten years earlier! That evening the children put on a program demonstrating their learning in the Sunday School for the last year, followed by a party complete with sausages, buns, ice cream, and special drinks.

I had eighteen or twenty for the class dealing with children's ministry. We met all morning in the town hall, ate lunch at the church, met again for three hours in the afternoon, ate dinner back at the church, and had class for an hour-and-a-half in the evening. We knew we had done something by the end of the week!

On Saturday, the Gerszenyis took me back to Budapest where we did a bit of sightseeing in that beautiful city on the Danube before I boarded the train to return to Vienna. I wish I could have seen more of the city, but time wouldn't permit.

In 1993, I went to the Haus and taught again. Following the class at the Haus, I went to Romania to teach a class. The class was conducted in eastern Romania in what had once been a resort hotel. The economy was such a wreck that business had dried up for the resorts, and TCM could rent the sleeping and meeting rooms for a very reasonable price.

I took the train to Arad on the eastern Romania border. There a TCM representative picked me up and took me to a hotel for an overnight stay. The next day a couple took me to the final destination. I had eighteen to twenty in the class. We had an enjoyable time together but had to work most of the time because we were finishing at dinner on Friday. Some of the students took me out one day after lunch so I could see the immediate area which had been a vacation spot for Ceausescu who had removed the top of a beautiful mountain to build a vacation palace and a helicopter pad. The class finished, I rode with three students back to Arad where they delivered me to the hotel.

The next morning I was to take the train back to Vienna. It was a challenge to find the train. I had taken a taxi to the railroad station. When I got there, I couldn't find anyone who could speak English. The departure/arrival board was in Romanian, though I thought I had figured out the track number for the train I was to take. I went there, but the train appeared to be heading in the wrong direction. Two women approached me. They were also trying to figure out the right track. Among us, we spoke English, Romanian, German, and a couple of other languages. By working back and forth, we finally figured out we were at the right place and huddled together until time to board. And off we went to Budapest and on to Vienna.

Another Academic Challenge

The North Central Association (now the Higher Learning Commission) relies on peer evaluators to uphold their standards. The evaluators are chosen from applicants and nominees from the member schools. A team is usually four in number for schools the size of CBS. I was encouraged by some at CBS to apply to be a peer evaluator. I did, and I was appointed to the peer evaluation cadre.

My first visit was to a small fundamentalist Bible college in Wisconsin. The team was led by a very competent dean from Olivet Nazarene College. He was helpful to me and intent on helping me succeed in this new role. I very much enjoyed the experience and looked forward to future trips.

The first visit still elicits a chuckle when I think about it. It was super conservative both theologically and in lifestyle. The students had a long list of specific rules to guide virtually every action. One was that if a boy and girl walked together to church or downtown, they had to walk a prescribed route—no shortcuts, no back streets, only the prescribed path that could be witnessed by many people. When we met with students, someone asked about the plethora of rules. Specifically, he asked why the prescribed route was so important. One young man answered, "Well, you know how boys are." He certainly didn't have a high view of the morality of his gender!

Over the years I made two visits to schools in Arkansas, two in Oklahoma, one in Michigan, one in Iowa, and one in Indiana in addition to the Wisconsin trip, and also served as a reader evaluator for a couple of schools. In 1993-94, I chaired my first two teams, a greater responsibility that I enjoyed.

The visit to Indiana deserves expanded description. We were to visit a non-traditional school in the African-American community on the near east side of Indianapolis. The school was led by a priest. The Dean was a nun, not especially competent, but she was a loyal devotee of the priest. The school had its beginnings as an adult education outreach of the Roman Catholic parish. Over time they added college level classes and became a full-fledged college appealing to adults who likely would not have attended other colleges in the metropolitan area. They were accredited, but they wanted to add a psychology/counseling degree and a graduate program in inner city ministry. They had been denied the psychology program in the previous visit—and they were irate about it. Racially laden letters had been sent to the North Central office. One letter accused the previous team of racial discrimination even though one member of the team was African-American. But in their terms, he had turned Uncle Tom.

Fortunately, we had an exceptionally skilled chair for the team. We met for Sunday evening dinner with the President, Dean, and director of the inner city ministry program and had a congenial conversation. It turned out that the director of the graduate program was a Disciples of Christ minister who had been encouraged at one time to attend CBS. He hadn't been able to, but he maintained high regard for CBS. That put him and me off to a good start.

The school had worked hard on the psychology degree, and the psychology professor on our team—she was an African-American—related well to those in her area of inquiry. I was able to affirm the inner city ministry degree. The team could recommend permission to pursue both degrees. You would have thought we were the great white knights who had ridden in to rescue them from some evil force! When I was ready to leave, the President escorted me to my car, expressed deep appreciation for how well we had listened to them, and invited me back as his guest at any time. It was quite the opposite reaction from what I had been afraid it could be!

Ministry at Mt. Washington

I first began my part-time ministry at Mt. Washington Church of Christ (now Parkside Christian Church) in October

1981, the first fall I was in Cincinnati. Mt. Washington was on the east side of the city and had grown numerically in recent years. It was led by a talented young pastor, Steve Reeves, who wasn't yet thirty years old. He had been the youth minister first, but had been urged to become the preaching minister when the minister with whom he worked resigned. A youth minister was on the staff full time. However, the Sunday School and other Christian education programs needed to be focused, and volunteers needed to be recruited and trained. Those were my jobs as well as to help the leaders develop a vision for Christian education. They were not in a financial position to add another full-time staff person. The answer could be a part-time experienced minister. The young minister learned from his mother, who worked at Standard Publishing Company, that I would be moving to Cincinnati. He jumped on the information and contacted me to determine my interest. When I went to Cincinnati to buy a condo, I also spent time with him and the chairman of the elders hammering out details of the position. I decided to accept it and looked forward to working with a good church.

Mt. Washington was a good church. The pastoral leadership was strong, and the eldership was composed of committed, able individuals. Many fine teachers worked in the Christian education program. I developed cordial relationships with every teacher but one who objected to a woman being on the staff.

The church averaged just over 500 for worship, but only a bit over 300 for Sunday School. A couple of adult classes were doing well, but most needed a lot of improvement, especially in outreach to potential new class members. That was a major part of my work. I remained on the staff until the end of June 1984 when I left to make my lengthy trip to Papua New Guinea. But Mt. Washington was still my church, a place with good friends and supportive Christians.

Meanwhile, the pastor asked me to develop a class for older single women. We surveyed the membership and found that we had 60 single women ages 35 to 65. Most of them were not in any kind of small group to further their Christian lives. We set out to work to establish the class. We had fourteen who committed themselves to being involved in a Bible class designed for them. On the appointed kickoff day, we had twelve in attendance. Though the class was never large—probably fifteen at most—it was an incredible ministry, meeting some deep needs of the participants. The fellowship was a strong feature, and the women were very good at ministering to each other. It was one of the best experiences I had ever had in a church. I made good friends from among the members—and have stayed in contact with several of them all these years.

The minister resigned, and a new minister was called in 1987. Shortly after he became the minister, the elders asked to meet with me. They wanted me to return to the staff to continue the work I had been doing three years before. I agreed and returned to the staff for two years. I did what I could and was involved in planning for new facilities that later became reality. However, it was not a good fit working with the new minister. Life was increasingly hectic at CBS. So I resigned and decided to leave the congregation because I didn't have a lot of confidence in the senior minister.

My new church home was a new congregation being planted in northern Kentucky. I sold my condo and bought one in Wilder, Kentucky. A woman by the name of Phyllis Florence and I shared responsibilities in planning and leading Christian education. This was a wonderful opportunity to get the Christian education in a new church off on the right foot. I remained there from the fall of 1991, until I moved to Tennessee in the summer of 1994.

Developing a New Degree Program

For several years, some, mostly friends and alumni of the school rather than faculty, had encouraged the development of a professional counseling degree to prepare licensed counselors in Ohio, one of the two most demanding states in which to achieve licensure. However, by 1990, we were ready to work on it. We wanted a high quality program, but we didn't want so many in the program that it would fundamentally change the nature of the seminary. The first step was to find a faculty member. We found the right person. She was a licensed clinical psychologist and in private practice, but wanted to teach. She had a Ph.D. in clinical psychology. She was sympathetic to our concerns for what we wanted in a program. She had several credits from the undergraduate school before she had seriously pursued her degree in psychology. And she was tenacious, extremely important as we entered this project. Her tenacity first had to be demonstrated in the interview/call process which was long and sometimes contentious. In the end she was called and we could proceed.

Then the curriculum had to be shaped to reflect theological content as well as professional competence. Certain prescribed professional courses were given from the Ohio Board of Regents which must approve the degree; others were essential as far as the seminary was concerned. We achieved the balance and came up with a sixty-hour Master of Arts in Counseling. The Ohio Board of Regents approved the degree, and we were ready to recruit our first students to enter in the fall of 1993.

We had decided to limit the initial class to fifteen. We had about twenty good applicants. Each applicant was interviewed, and the final fifteen clearly emerged. At the same time, a counseling center had been established on campus where students could gain some of the practical experience needed for licensure. Part-time faculty members were also identified and hired on a course-to-course basis.

It was a long, sometimes tedious, too often contentious process. But it was a proud moment when the program was up and running with good students—and with generally good support from the college and seminary community. It was due, I believe, to careful planning. And it has been a strong program ever since.

The Beginning of the End

I had my hands full, no doubt about it. Dean. Coordinator of the retention program. Administrator of the faculty development program. Teacher. Liaison for accreditation matters. Director of the assessment program. Conductor of workshops among the churches. Any one of the duties could have profited from more attention. But the areas of responsibility were being carried out well in large part because I had an incredibly able secretary, Arletta Paddock, who would see any project to a finish. Had it not been for her, my office could never have done the work with excellence.

My areas were going well, but life on campus was anything but peaceful. The President was at loggerheads with trustees, the undergraduate Dean, and the Director of Development who left a year after the President came.

A new development director was hired—a man who appeared to be very promising, based on his previous experience and his interview. He seemed to be a soft spoken man who claimed that he was devoted to the school and desired only to raise money for the school. However, I'm not sure that he ever raised much money. And though I don't know this for sure, I've always thought he was the pick of the trustees to become the one to be sure that the trustees had enough on the President to fire him. From within a month after Ed set foot on campus, nothing was peaceful again.

First the chief financial officer was fired. No good reason—he was doing a good job. But I know that the President later apologized to him, and the President himself told me that he felt in retrospect that he had been manipulated into the decision.

The President held a Ph.D. in speech and debate, and he relished debates about potential courses of action. I always got along well with him in debating through issues. He didn't mind if you disagreed with him so long as you would think through the situation. But that was anathema to the new Director of Development and the Dean, both of whom were upset beyond reason when someone disagreed with them. That extended beyond the President to anyone else with whom they worked: you were expected always to agree with them.

At the end of the 1992-93 school term, the President was fired, and the development director was named the interim president, a position he held for eight months. He then ruled by fiat and fear.

He called me to his office the day after he assumed his responsibilities. His opening remark when I went in was, "I don't think you like me. You never agree with me." I was shocked. I explained that I did not dislike him, but that I considered it a part of my job to point out various facets of a problem or potential solution. But it became evident in the conversation that I was never again to express a view dissenting with his.

At the same time, he said, I had to quit traveling so much; it was costing the school too much. Come to find out, he had concluded, without determining the facts, that the school funded every trip I made—to accreditation sites, churches, wherever. The fact was that the school had funded only two trips for me that year—one to the annual accreditation meeting where I represented CBS and one to Vienna to teach at TCM where I also carried out school responsibilities to monitor the contractual program we had with them. I provided documentation for him, listing every trip I made that school year and who had funded it.

The gist of the conversation was that he was boss and that he would be rid of me, no questions asked, if and when he wanted to. I left his office quite certain that I had to pursue another place of employment, as much as I didn't want to.

It wasn't many days later when the Dean of Students came to see me. He had been threatened as well. But he came to tell me that I should keep an eye on my back, for the interim president had told him that he thought the school would be better off without me.

I have always believed that he would have fired me that summer had we not been completing our self-study for a visit in April 1994.

Later the self-study became his gripe. He wanted us to include no evaluations of weaker areas. Nor did he want us to include any recommendations for improvement. I tried to reason that not mentioning obvious areas of need would not be overlooked by the accrediting team. I was saved from that problem, however, for the trustees named a new president who would assume office January 1. I met with him and explained my dilemma. He, of course, told me that we needed to include weaknesses as well as strengths and that he would be sure I was protected from the interim president's wrath.

I began the job search, something I had never expected to do again. And the Lord was faithful, as He had always been.

One evening I had left the interim president's office after an especially threatening session. (This was a week or two before the new president was named.) I remember driving across the city to home that evening weeping and saying, "Lord, what am I to do? What am I to learn from this?" And that very evening I had a call from Calvin Phillips, the president of Emmanuel School of Religion (now Emmanuel Christian Seminary) to talk to me about a position there. The Lord timed that encouragement perfectly!

I realized that I had to select my next place of service carefully. I was fifty-four years old and should think, I believed, that I could make only one more move. Fortunately, the Lord provided choices. I was contacted by a church in Indiana, which held some interest for me, and by three colleges—Lincoln Christian College and Seminary, Johnson Bible College, and Hope International University. I soon crossed Johnson and Hope off my list, for I couldn't get a clear picture of what they wanted me to do. The church too was eliminated from my list: I didn't think I would be content in that situation for several years. So the choice boiled down to Lincoln or Emmanuel.

I mentioned that I met with the new president before he took office. David Grubbs is a man whom I respect highly and would have loved to have worked with. But it seemed to me that too much had occurred to mend fences for a productive decade before I retired. When we met, we discussed the accreditation issues mentioned earlier, and I told David that he was almost certain to receive my resignation within a short time after he became president and the reasons why I had reached that conclusion. He was wonderfully affirming, assuring me that he had no desire for me to leave, that he appreciated the contributions I had made to the school, and that he would support me in my work as long as I was there. I'm certain he would have done what he said, but in a way, he may have been relieved, for I learned about that time that he was receiving a lot of pressure to get rid of a woman as dean of the seminary. He had always told these dissenters, I am told, that he was supportive of me as dean and urged them to be supportive as well.

The appeal to go back to Illinois was a fairly strong pull despite my previous experience at the school. It was, after all, my alma mater. But I had, by this time, been to Emmanuel to teach nineteen times and I had made friends and respected the work there. It was a topsy turvy few months as I wrestled with the decision.

To complicate matters, Calvin Phillips had decided to retire as president at Emmanuel on May 31, 1994. I had lived through five administrative changes during my career, none of which had gone really well. So my question to myself was whether I wanted to take a chance on the transition not going well at Emmanuel. At the same time, I was stressed by the aggressive approach of the president at Lincoln, and I wondered if that was the face of things to come.

C. Robert Wetzel, who was Dean at Emmanuel during my negotiations, was the primary contact on campus. I found that I could always be candid with Bob about my questions. He encouraged me to interview both places so I could make valid comparisons. He was patient, calling now and again, but never setting deadlines for an answer.

I went to Lincoln to interview on probably the coldest day in January that winter. True to form, the wind was vicious on campus, making the wind chill factor bitter. A lot of snow was on the ground. At one point, I thought to myself, "I hated this winter weather in 1978. Why would I think I would like it any more now?" That wasn't the deciding factor, but it did make me pause to think.

I also went to Emmanuel for an interview. As rarely as it snows in East Tennessee, I drove in snow to get to Johnson City. But it was a typical East Tennessee snow—gone by noon the next day.

The interviews over, the wrestling over the decision continued. I explained to Bob my major reluctance to choosing Emmanuel, that is, who the next president would be. One night a few weeks later, I received a phone call from Dorothy Keister Walker, widow of the founding president of Emmanuel, and a good friend of mine. She was privy to the fact that Bob Wetzel would be the next president of Emmanuel. And though I took a bit longer to think over the decision, learning that he would take the leadership of the school was the deciding factor for me to choose to cast my lot with them.

I submitted my resignation about the middle of the semester. From then until the time school was out and I would go to TCM to teach in late May/early June, I was wrapping up my many responsibilities to hand off to whomever would next be responsible for them.

It was an emotional conclusion for me at CBS. I had been there for thirteen years and had expected to remain until retirement. Given a choice at the time, I never would have chosen to move. But circumstances interfered. I believe firmly, however, that the Lord guided me to the very kind of place I needed, again demonstrating his faithfulness.

And an important chapter of life closed. I could be grateful for the many opportunities I had been given, and I knew that I had given my work the best I had to give.

Chapter 8

EMMANUEL: THE PLACE TO BE

I moved to Johnson City, Tennessee in June 1994. As soon as school was over at Cincinnati, I made my annual trip to TCM to teach. I flew home from Austria, spent two nights in Cincinnati, collected the few things from my condo that needed to be taken in my automobile, and drove to Tennessee.

My furniture and belongings had already been delivered by the moving company to my new condo and office. The morning after I arrived in Johnson City, I began unpacking at my condo assisted by a friend and a young man from the seminary whom I hired to do lifting and heavy work. By the second day, I was settled in my residence and had done some unpacking in my office. That was finished off bit by bit the following week. I felt at home from the beginning and was glad to be relieved of the administrative hassles I had experienced for the past several years. I was sure I didn't want to be an administrator again.

I was scheduled to teach a summer session class for two weeks beginning the week after I arrived. I taught each morning from 8:00 until noon. After lunch I unpacked books and files until my office was as I wanted it.

I had one major project to work on that summer along with preparation for the two classes I was to teach in the fall. I had been designated to be the Fall Convocation speaker as I was installed as the new professor of Christian education. Obviously, I wanted to do well in that venue.

Life at Emmanuel

Emmanuel School of Religion had been established in the mid-1960s. It had initially occupied rented facilities at Milligan College. But the Pennsylvania Phillips family had built the current campus some years before.

At the time I arrived, the campus was made up of two buildings—the beautiful large granite stone building atop a hill across the street from Milligan, and also a caretaker's home located behind the main building. That changed over time with the addition of the Emmanuel Village composed of English-style cottages to provide student housing, the Fred and Dorothy Thompson Community Center, and the Ahlgrim Maintenance Building. But that was all close to a decade away.

Emmanuel had been led by only four presidents in its existence. Dean E. Walker served for a few years as President of Milligan and Emmanuel. Fred Thompson had led the school for fifteen years followed by Calvin Phillips' ten-year tenure as president. C. Robert Wetzel had begun his presidency June 1, 1994, a position he would hold for fifteen years.

Faculty came to Emmanuel and, by and large, stayed. There was occasional faculty turnover, but not often. My predecessor in Christian education, who also served as the Dean for many years, had retired. A long-time New Testament professor was preparing to teach only part-time in the future, and a new Boston University Ph.D. was replacing him that fall. The theology, church history, and preaching professors had been at the school for a decade or longer. A counseling professor had left a few years before. A new professor had been called, but he would not begin employment until 1996. A few part-time instructors joined us from time to time, usually teaching language courses.

The Emmanuel faculty and administration worked together congenially. That was true my entire time there. Faculty committees functioned well, making shared governance a pleasant experience and giving everyone a voice in most decisions. Faculty meetings were generally congenial, the Dean presiding, but the President in attendance. When major decisions such as faculty or curriculum matters were on the agenda, the "Walker Rule" prevailed. This meant that no major decision was made on the day the matter was presented. Rather it would be discussed, a motion made, and the action tabled for two weeks when the faculty met again. I saw again and again the wisdom of the rule. Not infrequently, objections or questions about a proposed action would arise. After the discussion and two-week wait for the final decision, it would almost always be a unanimous vote. The congeniality and mutual support was more than welcome after the stress of the previous few years.

The summer flew by, and before I knew it, school was started. I had a large Principles of Teaching class, a small second class. Emmanuel was also preparing for a joint visit the following spring from the Southern Association of Colleges and Schools and the Association of Theological Schools to affirm continued accreditation. President Wetzel had asked me to be the Director of Institutional Research and to pull together what had been done for the self-study, write the self-study, and handle the details of the visit. I had agreed.

Dr. Wetzel had been the Dean before assuming the presidency. His new position had left the deanship vacant. He appointed Bruce Shields as the interim dean for one year. In December, he appointed a committee to choose a permanent dean and opened the process for applicants and nominees. From the time Dr. Brown had retired from the deanship ten years earlier, four deans had served; none, with the possible exception of one, who really wanted to be Dean. They would consent to do the job for only a limited period of time so they could return to full-time teaching. This appointment would be for a permanent dean.

The President urged me to become an applicant for the position. I wasn't completely sure that I wanted to go back to administrative work, though I definitely missed some aspects of it. More than anything, however, I feared getting a fair evaluation for the job. The chairman of the board was the brother of the undergraduate dean at CBS—and that dean had passed on all kinds of prejudicial and false information about me. I finally told the president that I would be interested in the position, but only if I were to get an objective evaluation. I was assured I would.

The committee met one Monday morning in March. I knew they were meeting that morning, so I was surprised when the President came to my office about an hour after the meeting time. He explained what they had done and the applicants they had for the position. Then he said, "We made our decision, and we want you to be the Dean."

Frankly, I was surprised and overwhelmed and responded with perhaps the most stupid response of my professional life. "You're kidding!" I sputtered. He wasn't, of course, and reassured me that it was a real decision. We could then begin to work on a few details that we would continue to discuss until I began the job in June.

We had our accreditation visit in April, and accreditation was continued for another ten years. We had three notations on our ATS record. One of them was a carryover from ten years before. A high priority as I assumed the deanship was to focus on getting those removed in the next couple of years.

Dr. Shields installing me in the office of the Dean

I officially became Dean on June 1, 1995, though I was in Europe at the time. I had been committed to spending four weeks there in late May and early June. So Dr. Shields took care of any matters needing attention during that time. I had done some work ahead of time and could leave instructions for secretaries to carry out those tasks while I was gone.

We had a faculty opening to fill, as rarely as that occurred at Emmanuel. Early in the second semester, Rex Jones, the field education professor, had become ill and died before midterm. His work was covered by several different people for the rest of the semester. But we had to work seriously to fill that opening for the following year. One of the first things I did as Dean was to join with the Christian Ministries faculty to interview the person we wanted for the position. Mick Smith, an Emmanuel graduate and a long-time missionary, was interested in the position, but wanted to wait until the second semester to begin, when he would have concluded his dissertation for his D.Min. degree. We were willing to wait and hired a couple of part-time people to cover first semester classes. It was worth the wait, for Mick was able to shape his dissertation to revamp the Emmanuel field education program.

My first year as Dean went as smoothly as I could have wished. I had a learning curve, of course, finding out how things were done at Emmanuel and determining procedures that could be improved and more effective. I taught a class each semester and one in the Wintersession.

One of the tasks I wanted to get done as soon as I could was to add a degree in Christian education. I was thinking of a Master of Arts in Christian Education or the Master of Religious Education degree. However, faculty generally favored a M.Div. in Christian Education. They reasoned that the person leading Christian education in a congregation should be as well prepared in Bible and theology as the preacher. I was convinced of their point of view, and we added the degree.

Our faculty handbook had been well crafted in the beginning. But it was quite far out of date, and it left some matters fuzzy and ill-defined, especially how a tenured faculty member could be terminated. A handbook revision had to be completed. It was a year-and-a-half project. We embarked on the journey and completed the project with a much more usable handbook.

The issues of advancement and termination of faculty pointed up the inadequacy of our faculty evaluation system, which rested entirely on student class evaluations on a home-made form. That had to be changed as well. In the end, we adopted a faculty evaluation system that was a near duplicate of the one developed at CBS. At Emmanuel, however, we utilized both junior and senior faculty evaluators, a change that I think strengthened the system.

Accrediting associations were pushing harder and harder for schools to develop outcome assessment plans that demonstrated that the stated educational goals were being achieved. That required careful review of preset goals and stringent evaluation of academic programs. We developed a plan that included surveys of every graduating class using a form that gave comparative data with graduates from other schools. We also administered each year a survey to every graduate from five years previous, compiling the results for each degree program. We also decided to do a lengthy review of each program every five years using data we had collected plus a day-long meeting with a representative group of graduates from that degree program. These day-long meetings were treasure troves, producing the kind of input we needed to make informed curricular changes. Both the M.A.R. and M.Div. programs were beneficiaries of this work.

By the end of the second year after the accreditation visit, we had removed all of the notations against the school in the ATS file. Our assessment plan was showing its worth, and our curricular revision was well under way.

In the absence of a counseling professor, I took up a duty that I would have assigned to him or her. Someone from Emmanuel was needed to serve on the CPE committee that supervised and evaluated the CPE programs at the Johnson City Medical Center and the Veteran's Administration hospital. Several Emmanuel students were in the CPE program every year; we needed to be a part of the oversight of the work. I took on that responsibility until the counseling position was filled. That led also to opportunities to work on other community-based health care/spiritual support activities. As a result of this work, I became convinced of the critical nature of CPE training for pastors and worked with the curriculum committee to work that into our degree changes.

I was also invited into community involvement, first as a board member for the Appalachian Council of Girl Scouts of America, a position I held for several years. The Johnson City evening Rotary Club wanted someone from Emmanuel to be a member of their club. The President was a member of the larger Tuesday noon club, so he asked me to join the evening club. I did and found it an enjoyable association. In 2002 I left the deanship and was employed overseas part of the year, making involvement in Rotary impossible any longer.

First Christian Church

When I think of Johnson City, I think as much about my church as I do the seminary. I moved to Johnson City determined that I would visit at least three different churches before I made a decision of where to place my membership. I didn't fulfill that promise to myself, however. The first Sunday I went to First Christian Church with a good friend of mine. She invited me to go with her and her friends for dinner. It turned out that six to eight single ladies ate Sunday dinner together almost every Sunday. If a person wanted to go, the requirement was to appear at the front door to meet the rest of them following the second worship service. They would choose the restaurant for the day and proceed to it. If a person chose not to go or couldn't go that Sunday, she simply wouldn't appear. I liked the church and enjoyed the dinner group. I was so satisfied with what I found there that I felt no need to look further. I placed my membership at the church by the end of July.

It was that summer, even before I had placed my membership at the church, that I was asked to be a part of the committee that planned and oversaw women's ministry. They had, just the year before, changed from the traditional women's circles to Bible study groups. They had made the mistake of trying to make each Bible study a clone of the others. This hadn't worked as well as they had hoped. I think I was some help to them in reshaping the studies somewhat. We decided that the primary focus was Bible study, but each group could shape itself as it wanted to emphasize specific activities such as prayer. A new group was added—and I was asked to be the leader. I led that group for the next eighteen years!

The leadership group had decided to have a kick-off luncheon in late August to recruit enrollees for the various groups. I was asked to be the speaker. This event was a huge success, and enthusiasm for the women's ministry was high. The model developed that summer shaped the women's ministry for the next fifteen years.

Don Jeanes, the minister, asked me also to put together a task force to examine the church's adult Sunday School program and to develop plans for the future. The church had three strong Bible classes, two that had waned in recent years but still ministered well to existing membership, two classes that had potential they weren't realizing, and a class or two that were small and generally ineffective. The task force decided that a new class would be quite helpful.

The strategy for starting a new class was to offer a year-long elective Bible survey class. This, we thought, would improve biblical literacy for any who wanted to take it, at the same time identifying potential candidates for a new class. I would teach the class during the first teaching hour on Sunday. The response to the class was overwhelming. About forty people enrolled and most were faithful to the end. Several of those involved had not previously been involved in an adult Bible class. Several others took time out from one of the less effective Bible classes, though they intended to return to their original class at the end of the survey course.

The survey class worked exactly as we hoped. A nucleus for a new class emerged, and we made plans to begin the new class in September 1996. One of the less effective adult classes was motivated to aim toward significant improvement after having been alarmed at so many who opted to take a year out of the class.

Beyond the nucleus, we identified a couple who would help provide leadership for the class. I would teach, but Roger and Linda would facilitate fellowship, handle absentee follow up, and care for Sunday morning details.

We also identified potential members and contacted them to invite them to be a part of this new venture. We made no overture to anyone who attended a class regularly. We decided to name the class Anchor, a solid name with no indication that it was for singles or married, men or women. Anyone in nearly any situation could feel comfortable, and we wanted this to be an inviting group for both men and women and for older singles.

The Anchor class was born the second Sunday in September 1996. We had expressed interest or commitment from about 25 people, but on the first day about 35 attended. After a few weeks, attendance settled into the mid-twenty range. From the beginning it was a diverse group with a few more women than men, about one-fourth single, and an age range of 35 to 70 years of age. Several people who once had attended Sunday School but had quit for one of any number of reasons attended. Several newcomers to the church who hadn't yet found a group to which to belong also joined in.

The Anchor class was built to achieve specific purposes. The first was to provide sound biblical instruction. We studied from the biblical text, not depending on some poplar modern author's book to set the agenda or answer all the questions. The second purpose was to do Bible application of the study to the learner's life. A lesson needed to do more than merely convey information for the sake of information. The third purpose was to serve as a fellowship base. Fellowship was understood to mean social activities, but much more such as helping bear burdens for each other, praying for each other, caring for the sick and grieving, and generally being present in the lives of those entrusted to their care. The final purpose was outreach. We were never to be happy as we were: we were to actively seek others to share with us.

The class has by and large lived by the purposes set out from the beginning. I figured out one day that at least thirty deaths of close relatives occurred over the first fifteen years of the class history, each eliciting appropriate and sometimes sustained acts of support. People have been assisted by class members. Offerings have been taken to meet a financial need for someone. People have provided rides to therapy or doctor's appointments. Meals have been provided for those recovering from surgery or other hospitalizations. They have provided thousands of dollars to buy rice for the hungry in India. They have developed a caring, helping community. And I can verify it firsthand: they have served me at times of need. They have been family to me. I taught that class for sixteen years—up to the Sunday before I moved from Johnson City. In many ways, it may have been the best ministry of my life.

I was also on the committee for the first two all-church women's' retreats and led Bible studies for probably the first four of those retreats. I taught Wednesday evening classes a few times. In short, I was deeply involved in the church. This was my family, my church, my frame of reference for ministry outside the seminary.

A Battle of a Different Kind

Back in 1992, I had discovered that I had ocular histoplasmosis, a retinal condition that causes blood vessels in the retina to burst and bleed. Vision is occluded and then begins to diminish. I discovered something was wrong one Saturday in April 1988 when I was doing a teachers' workshop north of Cincinnati. We were meeting in an interior room with no external light source. There was an emergency light source identified by a large red light. I was showing a filmstrip on discipline to the teachers. While the recorded narration was playing, I closed each eye just to see what I could see with the other eye. Surprise! I couldn't find the red spot with my left eye. On Monday I called my ophthalmologist to check this out. He dilated my eyes and determined there was a problem he could not deal with. He made an appointment with a retinal specialist at University Hospital for the next day. I went, had my eyes dilated again, and underwent a test when the doctor injected a dye into my system and then took a series of pictures to trace the dye. And he found the problem. I made an appointment to return to see him, and he repeated the test to pinpoint the place of the leak. At the time the only treatment was a laser treatment, which, of course, would cause a small loss of vision, but stop the bleeding. He said he could administer the laser treatment that day if I could wait until about 5:00 p.m. when he was finished with his appointments for the day. I could, and he took care of the treatment. I saw him every week or so to monitor any improvement. After all was said and done, I had twenty/eighty vision in the left eye, which the right eye could compensate for quite readily.

I used an Amsler Grid every day to check the vision. The grid is like a piece of graph paper. If the retina is healthy, looking at it registers dark straight lines. If the lines are squiggly, then something is wrong with the retina. In 1992, I saw the squiggly lines when I viewed the grid with my right eye. I quickly went to the doctor and he did the laser treatment. The spot was away off center vision so I had few leftover effects. And matters remained as they were until 2001.

In June 2001, I was in Bulgaria teaching. Using the Amsler Grid each day as I had for years, I found squiggly lines when I looked with the right eye. I was going back to Austria in a day or two and back to America in about ten days. So when I got to Austria and the problem persisted, I emailed my secretary to call the eye clinic and insist that I see someone on Monday. I even wrote out the speech she was to give them so they would understand the urgency for an appointment. When I saw the doctor on Monday, she affirmed that something was wrong and said I would have to see a retinal specialist for a diagnosis. I groaned inwardly, for I supposed I would have to go back to Cincinnati or to Vanderbilt in Nashville to see someone. But she assured me that an outstanding retinal specialist practiced in Johnson City and made an appointment for me on Friday. Life was not to be the same again.

It turned out that the retinal specialist was involved in clinical trials for a new treatment that had just been approved for the general public. It was so new that the insurance companies still hadn't ruled on whether or not they would cover it. He was certain after all the tests that I had a new outbreak of the ocular histoplasmosis. Since there was not yet approval from insurance companies and because what he proposed often worked, he injected a steroid shot directly into my rigye and made an appointment again for about ten days later.

Unfortunately, the steroid shot didn't work. But the new treatment had in those ten days been approved by my insurance company. He started the treatment that day. A treatment took two or three hours. It began with dilating the eyes and injecting the dye to pinpoint the spot to be lasered. Then a photosynthetic drug would be injected into my system with an IV. Following a ten-minute wait, a cold laser beam went into the affected eye for about fifty seconds. The theory was that the laser beam would draw the drug to the eye to begin healing the blood leak. The treatment had been developed in Switzerland and was now thoroughly tested in the United States. If needed, up to six treatments could be administered in sixteen months. And my vision did improve somewhat for a week or two after the treatment, but it would never last.

I had all six treatments between July 2001, and late October 2002. Finally the bleeding was fully terminated, but not before the best my vision could be corrected was 20/200. I could read almost nothing without a magnifying glass. I sought and bought all kinds of assistive equipment. I was fit with a binocular lens for my glasses. It would improve my vision to 20/50 to allow me to drive legally in Tennessee and almost every other state. I bought software for my computer that would enlarge anything on the screen from two to fifteen times and read to me. The doctor signed the form so I could get audio books from the Tennessee Library for the Blind and Physically Handicapped. That was a real life saver since I loved to read and had done almost none in over a year.

I'm grateful for the many who prayed for my vision to be fully restored. But I was frustrated by a couple of people who insisted I would be healed no matter what. As time went on and it seemed rather apparent that sight was not going to be restored, I often asked people to pray that I would have persistence and endurance to keep up my regular activities in spite of the visual limitations. Most honored that, but one person kept insisting there was no need for that prayer, for I would have vision restored. After the treatments ended and I was no better, she simply didn't address the subject all. I found that comforter not very comforting, but she was the exception to the rule.

On the whole, life wasn't curtailed too severely. At least I could learn fairly readily how to compensate for the visual loss. Since I was still teaching and wanted to continue for a time, I insisted that students submit assignments electronically. I would add all my comments and the grade electronically and return it to the student. It was a system that worked well.

My eye condition sensitized me to the needs of the disabled, and I became far more of an advocate for appropriate services for them in churches and schools. This advocacy was expanded somewhat a few years later when I broke my ankle. From that time on I needed to use a walker when my balance was affected because of the eyesight and the need for some kind of assistance as I walked. Yet none of these factors were problems that kept me from an active life and ministry.

Reflections on Emmanuel

No doubt about it: the Lord was clearly directing events and decisions that took me to Emmanuel. It was very much the right place for me—for many reasons.

Perhaps the major reason was that I was valued and affirmed as a woman in ministry. Women as valued partners in ministry was not merely an abstract concept; it was reality. Nobody to my knowledge ever attempted to pressure the President to appoint a male dean because a woman in that position was inappropriate or unbiblical. No faculty member ever balked at a decision on that basis. I was accepted for who I was—a female academic committed to the ministry of the church—never some kind of anomaly that had to be explained, hidden, or endured with a sense of embarrassment.

Emmanuel has an expansive view of the church, understanding the church to be far more than the local congregation on the corner. It is that, of course, and virtually every faculty person was a deeply involved member of the church they called home. But the church could no more be confined to that one expression than the wind could be controlled by human hands. The church was worldwide, and God's plan of redemption was at work in every corner of the universe. It is a great missionary call—one I had heard before, though not in the openness or expansiveness I heard here. With my long-term interest in missions, I was very much at home.

I experienced grace at Emmanuel. It was not a perfect place to be sure, and in general, people had no such expectations of others. It wasn't a cheap grace that permitted any kind of behavior among faculty, administration, or students. Occasional painful actions had to be taken, but never hastily, vindictively, or without prayer. Sometimes matters were solved with confrontation and talking out the situation. If we erred, it likely was in the direction of extending too much grace.

A faculty member—longstanding, an outstanding teacher and scholar—came one day to report that he was going to be facing a long, contentious procedure, most of the conflict to come over custody of his children. His wife had been unfaithful more than once in the marriage, but there was no reconciliation in sight this time. Where I had taught before he would have immediately been suspended from the classroom and would not have been offered a contract for the following year. But that wasn't the Emmanuel way. He was assured that his position was safe. He was relieved of committee and advising responsibilities for the remainder of the year to assure that he had time to deal with his personal problems and the legal procedures. The larger part of a faculty meeting was spent praying for him and his family. It was truly grace in action.

A serious problem came up with a student. Some of the accusations came from another student, the youth minister in the congregation where he preached. The accusations were moral in nature, though the evidence was largely circumstantial. Before any action was taken, the elders from his church were invited to meet with seminary personnel to ascertain validity of the charges. Some—especially involvement with pornography on the internet—appeared to be valid. Others involving a female student were apparently not true. When the student was then confronted, he confessed to an addiction with pornography, acknowledged the inappropriateness of some behaviors, and denied involvement with the female student as well as a couple of other charges brought by the youth minister. He was permitted to stay in school if he would agree to pursue counseling—he could choose the counselor if he wanted—and report regularly to the designated seminary official. He started out well, then began to miss appointments and fail to go to counseling. He finished the semester but was not permitted to re-enroll the following year. If we erred—and the youth minister clearly thought that we had—it was in the direction of grace.

One day our liaison with the Tennessee Student Aid Commission, which administered state and federal student loan funds distributed within the state, called me. He told me that an employee—and named her—had called and wanted to know some technicality about loan funds for a student who was not married to the person with whom he/

she was living. The state official affirmed that he knew that the Emmanuel policy was that students were expected to be married if they lived together. He simply wanted me to know that either the policy was being violated or that an employee was dabbling around where she had no business. (She had no authority to approve applicants, only to distribute funds as they came in.) I thanked him for his interest in the matter. I called in the employee to discuss the matter. She had been asking a question that dealt with her own family, though she was out of line to approach TSAC as she did. When I said that she should not have done this and could not be permitted to do it again, she claimed that she knew a situation like the one she had described among Emmanuel students. However, she could not (or would not) name who. In my previous place of employment, she would have been terminated on the spot for either of the offenses, that is, calling as an official representative of the school when she wasn't and withholding information of official policy from appropriate administrators. She was given two warnings: (1) she was never again to call TSAC as an official representative of the school about a policy matter and (2) she was obligated henceforth to report to the proper person a known violation of Emmanuel student life policy. We dealt firmly, but with grace, I believe.

Emmanuel allowed me opportunity to do two activities I loved—teaching and administration. And I was able to do both well without having to be imbalanced in life, doing more of one than the other. Some seasons found me heavily invested in administration, less in teaching. But another season saw that reversed. It allowed me to have a balanced approach.

Emmanuel gave opportunity to experience good shared leadership between faculty and administration. We had our share of misunderstandings, but the commitment to congeniality and grace helped us work them out. When two faculty members left the same year, the remaining faculty was edgy and quite suspicious that somebody in administration had caused their departures. Comments by the wife of one of those departing had thrown fuel on the fire. Even after the fall semester began and we had temporary replacements for the departed, the edginess continued. But we called a Monday afternoon meeting off campus and aired our concerns and exactly what actions had been taken. (Unfortunately, the reasons for leaving were a family situation that the faculty member didn't want known in one case and a moral situation in the other—both about which only the Dean and President knew and couldn't relate to others for ethical and privacy reasons.) An afternoon of discussion cleared the air, and we were back on solid ground.

Awhile later, a junior faculty member was denied tenure and told that he would not be offered a contract for the next year. He, of course, was upset, but the decision had been carefully made. It was a unanimous decision by the department and the committee on faculty advancement. This raised undue concern among faculty not involved in the decision-making process and among junior faculty who surely must have been wondering if the same thing could happen to them. This required another off campus afternoon airing of the problem. But it was accomplished, and life returned to normal. This would never have ended this well in my previous places of employment.

Changing Roles

I had become more and more engaged in mission interests and concerns as time went on. I had spent seven weeks at TCM in 1999, as a consultant to assist the Institute to achieve regional accreditation with the Higher Learning Commission. They were interested in my joining their staff. I had for many years intended to retire at age 62 and do mission work. So in the fall of 1999, I informed the president that I would serve as Dean and professor for three more years. The President affirmed my interests but suggested that we work out a shared position one-half time with each school. Over the next couple of years, he worked with the TCM president to work out the details. I would be half-time with TCM, though my work would be scattered throughout the year. I would spend from the end of May to the first of November in Austria. From December through May, I would be in Johnson City, though I would carry out some Emanuel tasks from Europe. At Emmanuel, I would still teach a course each Wintersession and spring term, be in charge of institutional assessment, and serve as accrediting liaison. I would be directly responsible to the President in both organizations.

I took an administrative sabbatical the summer and fall of 2000. One might call it a sabbatical anyway, though I was back and forth from Europe to Tennessee a few times. I left for the sabbatical the first of June. I worked there until the first of July before returning for ten days or so to attend the North American Christian Convention. I returned to Europe until the break in the TCM schedule in mid-August at which time I returned to the States to be present for registration and the first week of classes at Emmanuel. I returned to Europe the second week in September and remained there until the class schedule for the year was complete in early November.

From Vienna, I flew to Mumbai in India and spent three weeks in Kerala and Tamil Nadu, teaching at Christian Evangelical Fellowship in Kerala and Lakeview Bible College and Seminary in Chennai in Tamil Nadu. I left India a few days into December and flew to Seoul in South Korea. There I met with officials from Korean Christian Seminary who wanted to work out a cooperative arrangement with Emmanuel. While I was in Korea, I stayed with a good friend and her family on the Eighth Army Base where she served as a military chaplain. I returned to the States via San Francisco December 10.

My last three years as Dean at Emmanuel were as pleasant as my previous five years at the school. I could have been happy in that job for a good bit longer except for the urgency I felt to assist TCM in their accreditation process.

I left full-time employment with Emmanuel grateful for all that Emmanuel had contributed to me personally and professionally. It had been, in some ways, the best eight years of my life. And it was good to know that the association wasn't over. I would occupy the same office space, work alongside the same people, have the same concerns and joys as my colleagues with another set of relationships thrown into the mix.

This part-time Emmanuel, part-time TCM arrangement continued for three years. But when those three years ended, I still had the relationships at Emmanuel. I worked half time there with the same responsibilities as the previous three years and worked half-time at First Christian Church in Johnson City. I'll take that up later.

I taught my last class at Emmanuel in the spring of 2007. A new Christian education professor began work that fall. She would also do the institutional research piece of my job, so I maintained an office at Emmanuel and helped her learn the institutional research area. I retired entirely in 2008.

Chapter 9

A Six-Year Postscript

TCM

I retired as Dean at Emmanuel on May 31, 2002, and began the next day, June 1, as Dean of the TCM Institute. The half-time Emmanuel, half-time TCM would be my life for the next three years.

I was knee deep in accreditation issues both at Emmanuel and TCM. I put together the framework for the self-study at Emmanuel just before I left to go overseas. Once I arrived at TCM, I worked with the President to put together a framework for that self-study. But we needed to get started collecting a large amount of data that we had access to, though our computer system and procedures weren't as helpful as they could have been.

I had some in-country trips to teach that summer and fall. And at every two-week period when students were on campus in Austria, I was conducting focus groups with a random sample of the students to elicit student feedback and evaluation of the program. This proved to be a very profitable enterprise, gaining insights we could never get from a written survey.

We had other projects that needed to be completed before we could write a self-study. One was the production of a faculty handbook appropriate for our situation where we depended to a large extent on adjunct faculty. We had already done a good amount of work of faculty evaluation, but we needed to refine some aspects of it.

We had ten or twelve individuals who were designated as permanent faculty. They lived in Hungary, Belgium, Romania, Austria, Australia, and the United States. The faculty had never met as a faculty to do faculty business. We finally settled on a system: those designated as permanent faculty would gather at Haus Edelweiss in late August each year during the three- or four-week break in classes. We would begin on Tuesday and spend until Friday noon together dealing with typical faculty matters, carrying out the formal evaluation process, sharing writing and academic projects we were pursuing, and praying and doing Bible study together. I was involved in two of these meetings, and they turned out to be a time of renewal and good fellowship.

Of course, I had resigned as a board member for TCM at the spring board meeting. That action didn't change the need to be at board meetings, however; all administrators were expected to attend these meetings to provide insight and to answer questions related to their areas of work. I had always found these board meetings efficiently conducted, not wasting any time, but allowing for enjoyable times of fellowship and visioning for the future of the work. I would not have wanted to miss out on that.

My work at TCM took on a certain rhythm. When I was teaching, I didn't have time to do much else. But a pattern soon developed that allowed me to carry out my TCM work and at the same time keep up with responsibilities back at Emmanuel.

The TCM policy was that all staff members ate all meals in the common dining room when classes were in session. The exception was that everyone had a day off during each two-week class session and was free to skip the common meals if desired. The week between class sessions the dining room was closed, and we prepared our own meals. Each person also had two days off on the Saturday after students left, or on Monday, Tuesday, or Wednesday of the days following.

A typical work day for me would find me up at 6:30 and in the office about 7:15 to check email or to get started on other tasks for the day. The secretary usually came in a little after 7:30. We would walk together to the dining room for breakfast at 8:00.

I dried dishes after the meal. That was usually complete around 9:00, after which I would go about my day's work—teaching, observing classes, attending meetings, or dealing with tasks in the office, as the case may be. About 11:50, I went back to the dining room for lunch and again helped dry dishes after the meal. I usually conducted focus groups, one with the students from each country, about 1:30-2:30 on the two or three days we had them during a two-week period. Then it was back to my other tasks for the day until dinner at 6:00. And, of course, there were more dishes to dry in the evening. Kitchen work was done by 7:15. A night or two a week I joined a group visiting beside the pool until I was ready to retire for the day.

Although at that time TCM had ten employees and their families who lived there permanently and another four who lived there about half the year, the organization depended heavily on one long-term couple who served April-May, June-August, or September-early November, plus 14-16 short term workers who came for two weeks to volunteer their time and service.

One of the permanent workers oversaw maintenance. The short term workers serving in that area did mowing, weeding, painting, and occasionally bigger jobs based on the skills of the workers. Another long-term worker was the general manager and secretary. Another couple was in charge of guest services—cleaning, hospitality, helping students as needed. The male half of the team sometimes had another responsibility such as overseeing the upkeep and scheduling of automobiles. Another full-time couple was primarily engaged in support services for the Institute. She monitored and maintained the computer systems, and he handled logistical details for students such as travel arrangements, getting course plans and textbooks to students, and assigning classrooms. Another couple managed the kitchen, handling menu planning, food ordering, and food preparation. They had several short-term workers assigned to them during each session. The European Vice President completed the roster of permanent employees living at the Haus full time. After his children had started school, his wife worked in an area, which often changed from session to session based on need.

The campus was anchored by the enormous house called Haus Edelweiss. It was a three-story structure that had been restored to previous grandeur early in TCM ownership and was well maintained. Around most of the second story extended a balcony, kept beautiful and appealing with flower boxes in which something was always in bloom. A basement area had been finished as a classroom with a maximum seating of 20-25. The first floor featured a lounge area, the dining rooms (the original dining room, what had once been a porch area that had been enclosed, and two smaller rooms that could seat a few if the dining room was overflowing), restrooms, a tiny office for the guest services directors, and kitchen and food storage areas. A few years before a large classroom had been attached adjacent to the kitchen. The classroom could accommodate up to 35 students. The second floor in the original house had an apartment, an efficiency apartment, showers, and a room that was sometimes used for a class of no more than 15. Over the classroom that had been attached to the kitchen, there were two apartments for visiting faculty. The third floor in the original house had a couple of apartments and a dormitory style sleeping area. Another small room on the third floor of the classroom/apartment attachment was used for small research classes.

On the original property purchased by TCM, there was the Gatehouse that now housed an apartment, the Cow Barn (its original function) that now housed a staff apartment and some student rooms, and just across the highway the Horse Barn (again its original function) to which a couple of additions and renovation had been made. The basement of the Horse Barn was a "shopping" area with clothing and other items provided by American churches for Eastern Europeans. The ground level had a large maintenance area on one end with an apartment to the north of it. (That is where I lived.) A conference room, copier room, and offices completed the first floor. The second floor housed the library, a lounge for students, and rooms for male students.

In 1989, a building known as the Leadership Training Center, had been built a few feet east of the Haus. The basement area was a classroom/chapel that could seat a group of any size that would be at the Haus, restrooms, a storage area, and a kitchenette. The second floor housed two staff apartments. The third level was guest rooms occupied by the short-term workers.

Two houses in the neighborhood that bordered the campus on the south completed the campus. One house, about a block from the main campus, housed the European Vice President's family. The other, a half-block nearer, had a couple of apartments in it.

The largest number of students that we could accommodate in the early 2000s was 60-65. Not all groups were that large: sometimes students ran into snags getting a visa to study abroad. With 60 students, 30 faculty and staff, and 14-16 short-term workers, over 100 gathered at meals. That called for work—lots of work—to care for rooms and food preparation.

Short-term workers were volunteers from churches all across America. They often used their vacation time to volunteer their service. They were usually assigned to one of three major areas of work—kitchen, maintenance, or guest services. Now and then, someone with a special skill would be assigned to a task demanding that ability. Volunteers left the United States on Thursday and arrived in Vienna by noon or shortly after on Friday. They had time to get settled in their rooms and take a walk or nap before dinner. A couple of staff families were assigned to join them for dinner and begin the orientation process.

Orientation for short-term workers began in earnest at 9:00 on Saturday morning with a tour of the campus and general information they would need to know. Following lunch, at which time they would be joined by all the staff, they would go with their work supervisor for more specific orientation. They finished mid-afternoon to allow time for rest. Dinner followed, and the evening was free. Often short-term workers who had been there before would introduce the new workers to the pastry delicacies at the stift at the fifteenth-century monastery at Heilengenkreuz.

On Sunday, a staff family was assigned to the short-term workers to take them on an outing for the day. They were provided a sack lunch if they wanted it, but most chose to buy their lunches wherever they were so they could sample Austrian cuisine. Outings were to places like Schonbrunn Castle in Vienna, the abbey in Melk combined with a ride through the Danube valley, or perhaps something a bit further afield. The choice belonged to the host couple. They returned by 5:30, in time for dinner followed by a worship service.

Orientation was completed by noon on Monday, and students began to arrive that afternoon and sometimes early evening. After dinner on Monday, staff, short-term workers, and students met in the chapel for student orientation and prayer.

From Tuesday morning onward the schedule was different than it had been in the early days of leadership training when classes were not for credit.

Breakfast was at 8:00 a.m. Every other morning it was a European breakfast—rolls, cheese, and ham and turkey deli meat with juice, coffee, and/or tea. The students assigned to kitchen duty for the day dried dishes and reset tables for lunch until time to go to class. The morning class sessions lasted from 9:00 to 10:30. After a fifteen-minute break for coffee or tea, classes met again from 10:45 to noon. Lunch was at noon. Classes convened again at 3:00. At 4:30, a break was planned, followed by class from 4:45 to 6:00. After dinner, the time was free for students to study or do what they wanted.

Short-term workers usually worked at their jobs until about 3:30, after which they could take a short break or visit a class. The kitchen workers would return about 5:15 to finish dinner preparations. Guest services workers would report to the dining room about 5:30 to fill water glasses, put milk and butter on the tables, and make coffee. Maintenance workers would report to the dish room to do pots and pans. It was all like clockwork. The rhythm of the day defined life.

Students had classes on Tuesday, Wednesday, and Thursday. On Friday, the cadence changed: we had a day off from classes. After breakfast, the students were given a sack lunch and taken to Shopping Center South where they could take the free bus to downtown Vienna if they chose. An hour or so later the short-term workers were taken to the shopping center for a bus ride into Vienna. The staff joined together at noon to eat leftovers from previous meals. One couple was assigned to campus duty that afternoon while the others got a few hours off. By 5:00, drivers were transporting short-term workers and students back from the shopping center. The class schedule resumed on Saturday.

Breakfast was at 8:30 on Sunday, followed by worship at 10:00. What inspirational services! Frequently a professor preached. Almost always the national groups had prepared a special musical presentation. Communion time was always profoundly moving for me: we saw the global nature of the church. Presenting the meditation might be a Belarussian believer. Praying at the table might be a Bulgarian and an Estonian. Serving the emblems could be an American, a Romanian, a Czech, and a Moldovan. I never failed to get goose bumps as I was reminded again of the universal nature of God's love and redemptive offer.

Worship was followed by a photo-op session. A group picture including staff, students, and short-term workers was made. Of course, everyone wanted a picture, so that frequently meant fifty or sixty pictures were snapped. Sunday dinner was always special with an extra-special dessert. Sunday afternoon retained the longtime practice of taking students and short-term workers to Baden to enjoy a concert in the park, a climb to the Roman ruins, or a taste of Austrian pastries or ice cream. It was back for dinner at 6:30, and a free evening.

The regular class schedule was followed on Monday, Tuesday, and Wednesday. Classes met on Thursday morning, students taking exams in the classes requiring it, others presenting final projects or papers. Following lunch, everyone gathered in the drive for a very large prayer circle. We often heard words of thanks from students extended to staff and short-term workers as well as professors. A few were selected to voice our prayers, and the goodbyes began. That was always another profoundly moving time: I still stifle a sob when I think about it. Students then began to depart, some in cars, some to train or bus stations, and an occasional one to the airport.

The staff and short-term workers then began a harried effort to clean guest rooms, do laundry, remake beds, clean the kitchen fastidiously, and in general clean every nook and cranny of the facilities. They completed the work, usually by mid-afternoon on Friday. Short-term workers and staff that wanted to go then went to a nearby very nice restaurant to enjoy a closing celebratory meal together before short-term workers departed the next day.

So the beat went quite predictably, although every set of classes had its share of surprises.

My work certainly involved interaction with short-term workers, staff, and students. But the first summer was consumed with putting together the documentation we needed to submit to the Higher Learning Commission to allow us to go forward to pursue candidacy status. We had to submit a load of documentation. The Higher Learning Commission had the authority to accredit overseas programs offered by an entity in their area (Indiana), but they had yet to have done so. That meant that we had no institution's work to produce a model or advise. And being a school that was non-traditional and served people from many countries, we had some unique issues to document. For example, students sometimes graduated from high school earlier than in the States, sometimes having three years of high school rather than four. We had to document how their secondary school education was equivalent to a high school diploma in the United States. We had to document that we had the authority to offer classes in any country where we conducted them. We had a good graduate library in Austria, but students often needed material in their own language and available in their own country. We had to document libraries where we had working relationships for students to use what they needed. All of this was possible to do, but it was slow. We had to submit the report a second time to add additional required details. But we finally received permission to proceed to the self-study phase. And we moved full speed ahead.

Back at Emmanuel, we were also preparing for our ten-year joint visit from the Southern Association of Colleges and Schools and Association of Theological Schools. Both were imposing new standards, so we had to show we were in compliance with them.

Work with ATS

I had begun, even before retirement as Dean, to work with ATS. Over the years I did four or five visits to Michigan, Missouri, Pennsylvania, and Massachusetts, as I recall. I had been ready to go to North Carolina for another visit, but became ill with pancreatitis and was hospitalized a day or two before I was to leave. Needless to say, I didn't make the trip.

The invitation to make a five-year commitment to an ATS committee that was being funded by the Lily Foundation was even more challenging and interesting than the accrediting visits. A fifteen-member committee, joined by a half dozen ATS staff, was tasked with determining the lifestyle outcomes that should accrue from a M.Div. education that demonstrated graduates were ready for ministry. We met probably nine or ten times during the five years. We had productive meetings in appealing places like Chicago, Pittsburgh, Dallas, and San Diego. Our work produced two conferences for schools that had accrediting visits soon. And the work has informed later revisions to ATS standards. It was an honor to be a part of the committee and satisfying to make contributions to the work of schools throughout the United States. And, of course, the results of the work were helpful to the two self-studies I was involved in. One of the committee members turned out to be the chair for the ATS team that came to Emmanuel—a real bonus for us.

The End at TCM

When I had made the rearrangement of responsibilities at Emmanuel to become Dean at TCM, the TCM president had assured me that he would be supportive of the visual limitations I had. He had insisted that I could even invite a friend to come with me for the summer, no cost to the friend, to care for any needs I had. I distinctly recall his statement, "I'm not hiring you for what you can see. I want to access what is in your head." Something changed from 2002 to 2005, however—and I've never been sure what.

My work at TCM was going well from my perspective—and as far as I knew from everyone else's too. But as we began to write the self-study, I sensed that he had less and less confidence in me. One day in April 2005, I sent him a rough draft of a couple of chapters. The next day I got an email from him stating that I was making too many typing errors and that he was relieving me from my self-study responsibilities (though not all responsibilities as Dean).

We exchanged several emails—and the sense that he had lost confidence in me loomed larger in each exchange. I finally offered to resign, stating that I felt he had lost confidence in my work. He did not dispute that and accepted my resignation. He offered me a job to continue to teach and to be at the Haus, but I could get no specific duties I would carry out. I would have been very bored being at the Haus with no defined portfolio except to teach two or three times a year. I felt that, given my nature and work ethic, the only responsible action was to terminate my employment with them.

I flew to Europe in early June to complete a teaching assignment in Russia. I spent several days at the Haus wrapping up my work, passing along data for the self-study, transferring computer files to the right person, and saying my goodbyes. Other classes I was to teach that year and the next were canceled. I offered to teach each year and was scheduled for a 2007 date, but never again after that.

Leaving TCM was quite emotional. I had become deeply invested in the work as a board member, even before I was an employee, and the investment deepened over the three years as Dean. The Eastern European and Asian students had wormed their way into my heart. It would take some time to refocus, and I wondered if I would find anything else as deeply satisfying as my work with TCM had been.

First Christian Church

It didn't take long, however, for another challenge to emerge. Tim Wallingford, the pastor at First Christian Church in Johnson City, called to set a luncheon appointment. When we met, he asked me to consider taking the position of Minister of Adult Education at the church. My responsibilities, twenty hours a week, included supervision of adult Bible classes and planning and staffing offerings in the adult area on Wednesday evening. It was a good challenge, although it never lived up to the TCM challenge.

I tackled the job with enthusiasm, first visiting each class to observe what went on. I also met with leaders for each class to cast a vision of what they could be and do. We had several classes for adults. The largest and best organized was a class for senior adults. The average age was close to 80. They were a good class that became even stronger. The second largest class had been infused with new life in the previous couple of years. They wanted to be even better, making them easy to work with. The third largest class was a class with members mostly in their 40s. A couple in that class emerged as strong leaders to supplement the teacher's good work, and they matured into a fine adult Bible class. The next largest was the class I taught. They were easy to lead. Another class had its ups and downs, made some definite improvements, but never got on track. Another was simply resistant to change and remained the way they were. The Spanish class found it difficult to get on track too as did another class.

We needed some new classes. One was begun in the fall of 2006. It had a good start and served the needs of about two dozen people. We tried to add a couple more classes, but neither survived. The right leadership simply didn't emerge.

We had so many new members in the church with a low level of biblical literacy. I was convinced that the Bethel Series would be a good investment of time and energy. We enrolled as a congregation, and one of the associate ministers, his wife, and I went to Madison, Wisconsin for the training sessions. We recruited a very nice intensive study class that lasted the two years for which it was designed. That was followed by the congregational phase. Though we had a number of enrollees, the program was never really numerically successful at First Christian, mainly because the minister never really supported the program and refused to clear the Wednesday evening calendar of other studies in order to encourage people to take the Bethel class. People who enrolled really liked the study and gained much from it. You would have thought that by this time in my career I would have been smart enough to be sure the minister was fully on board. It demonstrates that we never know everything! And I still consider the time I spent teaching it a good investment of time.

Communication among classes was a strong need. I sent out a weekly newsletter to teachers and leaders in classes, keeping them up on what various classes were doing and trying to build teamwork. I usually included some kind of "training" piece in each letter in order to shape thinking about adult education. And, of course, occasional training workshops were held for teachers, and some we invited to attend because they had the potential of becoming good adult teachers.

Overall, we made progress with shaping classes to achieve the purposes of biblical instruction, biblical application, fellowship, and outreach. We averaged about 400 in adult classes each Sunday, and most classes were showing numerical growth. We sometimes reached as high as 450 in attendance.

I was also charged with planning the offerings on Wednesday evening. This was a much more frustrating endeavor. I would put together a good menu of classes, recruit teachers, occasionally teach a class myself, and begin to publicize what was coming. Then a week or two before the classes were to begin, the minister would insist on some major change—canceling a class he didn't want, adding one he wanted to teach, re-arranging the offerings for no apparent reason. And, of course, I had to double back and inform teachers that we didn't need them after all. It was a huge exercise in frustration.

I decided that I would resign my position at the church to coincide with the end of the last semester I would teach. By this time, I had been 48 years teaching in a college or seminary and/or ministering in a church. It was time to retire. Even then I continued to teach the Anchor class and for two years taught a Thursday morning Bible study for women. It was enough to keep me as busy as I wanted to be.

The decision to retire was made just in time. A week after I retired I broke my right ankle. That would have put a crimp in what I had been doing previously.

And so closed my professional career.

Chapter 10

COME TRAVEL WITH ME

Perhaps the best hours of my life have been spent traveling to many different countries to teach and minister. I have described some of those in detail. But I want to share additional travels and observations, so I have decided to bundle all those together in one chapter rather than dealing with each as it came chronologically. Country by country, I'll share highlights with you.

Russia

My first trip to Russia was in 1994. I arrived in Moscow on Sunday afternoon on a direct flight from Vienna. Alexei Fedichkin, the Russian national director for TCM, met me. His father Ben had been one of Gene Dulin's first Russian contacts. He drove me from Moscow to Vladimir where the class would be taught. We made a short detour on the way to visit his parents at their country dacha. Don't harbor grandiose dreams of this dacha. It was a one-room structure perhaps twenty by twenty feet and sparsely furnished—a bed, a few chairs and benches, and a table.

Alexei needed to change the wheels on his car. But we also took time to eat with Ben and Nina. The menu? Borscht, cheese, and bread. From there it was on to Vladimir.

Vladimir is one of three cities in what was known as The Golden Triangle connecting St. Petersburg, Vladimir, and Kiev. At one time it was the capital of Russia. The city is home to many ornate buildings dating back to the period when it was the capital.

I was supposed to have stayed in a small apartment for visiting professors in the large building where we would meet for classes. However, the apartment was not adequately finished so we had to make other arrangements. I ended up staying in a room in a hotel about six blocks from the center.

The hotel had long ago seen its better days. Draperies were faded. Rooms were simply furnished. It was drab. But the bed was comfortable and clean, and I spent little time there. A woman presided over each floor, knowing who came and went—and I suspect knowing everyone's business.

We first went to the house where the church met. The church moved to the new center. I met Valentina, a little wizened woman that I would have guessed to be eighty. I found out later that she was but sixty-nine. Her life had been hard. During World War II, she had been forced to go to Vladimir to work in the grain fields. After the war, she was forced to stay there to work in a tractor factory. She had moved heavy forms from place to place. It was no wonder she looked old! But she was a deeply devoted Christian, doing many good deeds for others all her life. She was a key member of the church. Alexei told me that nearly any business he visited in Vladimir was well acquainted with her and spoke highly of her. She was the cook for the week as we conducted the class.

Class began Monday after lunch. I had a rather large class—about 35—only a half dozen or less who were taking it for credit. Most were Sunday School teachers and youth leaders in their churches. They had come because of their devotion to their volunteer ministry.

We usually had high quality translators who were Christians and involved in their churches. This was an exception. Larissa was very good at translation, but she wasn't a Christian and was totally unfamiliar with the Bible. She expressed some interest in Christianity. One day she said, "I don't know the accounts you are using from the Bible. If I had a Bible, I would read those accounts before class and become familiar with them." You can believe, I am sure, that we found a Bible that was hers to keep!

I enjoyed working with Larissa who was retired from her job as a translator. We had many good conversations through the week, and I kept in occasional contact with her for a couple of years.

The day began with breakfast at the center. When the tables were cleared, we met in the dining room—the only finished room large enough to accommodate the class. Class began at 9:00 a.m. and continued until noon, with a tea break midway in the morning. We ate lunch at noon and took a break until about 3:00 pm. We met again from 3:00 to 5:00 pm followed by dinner. We met again from about 7:00-8:30 pm—and called it a day. Usually a couple of the younger women walked me to the hotel.

The women were all very curious about me. I encouraged them to ask whatever questions they had, even devoting a few minutes each day to that purpose. I don't remember all the questions, but they covered about every aspect of life.

A lovely lady, whose name I don't recall, usually helped Valentina in the kitchen to prepare the meals. She wanted me to come to her home one evening after class for a "light meal." I explained that she would have to arrange such an occasion with Alexei. Alexei loved to eat, so it wasn't difficult to persuade him. The gathering was arranged for Thursday evening.

A "light meal" it wasn't. The table was covered with food. I'm sure the lady had used her food money for much of the month to have so much food. And it was so good. Valentina was there as were a couple of women who were in my class. The ladies said, "You have let us ask anything about you that we wanted to know. Tonight you get to ask us anything you want to know about us." My question was, "How and why did you become a believer?"

The answers to my question were revealing. Valentina had been a faithful Christian from childhood to the present. The hostess had been reared in a Christian home, but had given that up for Communism and her career. But her life hadn't turned out well—she had an alcoholic husband from whom she was divorced. A few years earlier she had turned back to her childhood faith. Now she was trying to rear her granddaughter in the faith. The other two women were or had been married to alcoholics—and that bitter experience had turned them to the Lord. As I visited with other women in the class, I heard similar stories.

Alcoholism was pandemic in Russian culture. I was told that the life expectancy for men in Russia at that time was about 60 years while women had a considerably longer life span. The cause was attributed to the high rate of alcoholism among men.

We finished the class on Friday at 5:00 pm. Some students stayed overnight to go home the next day. Most, however, caught a train or bus to go home that evening.

On Saturday, Alexei's brother-in-law, Victor, came to drive me back to Moscow. He checked me in at a hotel where foreigners were permitted to stay. Then we set off to tour the Kremlin.

It was a nasty rainy day. The rain was heavy and we were sure to be soaked. But I didn't want to miss a tour of the Kremlin. We took in nearly every square foot of this amazing collection of buildings. We went to a part of the worship service of the Orthodox Church located inside the walls of the Kremlin. We were indeed soaked, but I didn't care.

The Kremlin in many ways surprised me. It was much larger and more formidable than I had envisioned. The large number of structures within the walls surprised me. And Red Square in front of the Kremlin was far larger than I expected. We visited another Orthodox Church as well as seeing several landmarks in the city. I would not have wanted to miss this day.

On Sunday morning, Victor picked me up, and we went to a church meeting in a building in the shadow of the Kremlin. It was the first of three services for the day. Later services would be held in the early afternoon and again in the evening, the latter service geared to young people. The church probably held about three hundred—and it was packed, as I was told it would be at the two later services.

The service lasted just over two hours. It featured several choir presentations, two sermons, prayers, and Scripture reading. Though I didn't understand Russian, I had a profound worship experience with these believers, many of whom had suffered a great deal for their faith. It was a fitting end for a grand week that I won't soon forget. I flew back to Vienna, arriving three hours late. I had to take a late night, for I needed to get laundry done so I could leave the next morning to fly to Sophia.

This first visit to Russia may have been the most fascinating for me. But each trip provided greater insight. On my second trip, I arrived on Saturday and worshiped with the church that by now was meeting at the center. Following the worship service, the pastor met with a group of women for lunch and Bible study. I was invited to join them.

The class went very well. It was not as large as the first class I had taught when I was there previously, but by this time participants were mainly credit seeking. I still had 15-20 in the class, however. I stayed at the apartment in the teaching center this time. Mike Crull, the European Vice President, came from Austria the last couple of days of the class to assess what yet needed to be done to finish the center.

On Saturday, Alexei took Mike and me to his home in a suburb of Moscow where we enjoyed a wonderful meal with him and his family. They were such gracious hosts. The next morning Alexei and his wife drove us to a church in Moscow where we worshiped. The church met in the basement of an office building. It was a relatively small congregation but had a meaningful worship service. Both Mike and I were expected to present a short message.

We had to leave before the worship service was completed, before the pastor preached his sermon for the day. We had a flight to catch and had to speed to the airport. Of course, the flight left late. Perhaps that was predictable: the flight for Vienna left late each time I was on it.

My third trip to Vladimir was in October. The drive from Moscow was beautiful with so many brilliant colors. Again

I had a class of fifteen to twenty and had a good time with the students. One of the students was Alexei's nephew who was a pastor in a city in far northeast Russia. His train trip home would take two days. Again I stayed in the guest apartment at the center. The surprise of the week was several inches of snow late in the week.

On Saturday, I had time to rest and do some sightseeing around Vladimir. Alexei's son Ben and nephew Timothy, who had been in my class, were charged with my care. They proved to be good hosts, even preparing an evening meal on Saturday and breakfast on Sunday. We departed on Sunday morning for Moscow and the airport. It was another good trip to Russia.

My final trip to Russia was in June 2005, the last in-country class I taught for TCM. Little differed this time from previous trips. The place was the same. I stayed in the same guest apartment. The class went very well. When class was over, I went to Alexei's home for a Saturday overnight before I returned to Vienna on Sunday. Again, Alexei and his family were gracious hosts. They expressed profuse thanks for the work I had done with TCM and with them and assured me that should I ever be in Russia again, I was to be a guest in their home. I left Russia with a warm feeling.

What is the future in Russia? Politically, I wouldn't want to predict. But there is an urgency for evangelism in some sectors. Many new churches have been planted. A contingent of young pastors and leaders has been, and continue to be, educated for ministry through the TCM Institute. Young pastors such as Constantine, Timothy, Ramone, and others have joined a corps of older pastors, many of whom are relatively new in Christ, to extend the work of Christ in Russia. What they are accomplishing for the Lord will bear fruit!

Ukraine

I made three trips to the Ukraine—and was scheduled for a fourth later in 2006 after I resigned. The first was in 1995.

A trip to the Ukraine began with a flight from Vienna to Odessa on the Black Sea. Some men from Kherson met me to take me by ground transportation about ninety miles northeast of Odessa. Considerable evangelistic activity had occurred in Kherson. A vibrant, growing new church had been planted and joined with the older more traditional church that had served the city for years. A certain amount of friction and mistrust had developed between the two churches, mostly because of the serious mistakes of a mission organization that had helped birth the new church. Those misunderstandings were rapidly dissipating by 2005, however, because TCM had taken the invitation to create a teaching center there. The President of TCM had wisely consulted first with the older church. He named a field director agreeable to the older church. Interestingly, the field director, who was everyone's choice for the position, was the pastor of the new church.

The Ukraine fascinated me. It was fertile land and once had been the breadbasket of Russia. But by this time the state-run cooperative farms were a failure. A passerby could see crops rotting in the fields simply because they couldn't or didn't get the harvest done in a timely manner. They were planting crops that produced well enough to feed the Ukraine and have grain to export. It was sad to see.

I was to be in the Ukraine for two weeks. I would teach a class for a week that invited as many from the churches as wanted to come. The second week the students and I would go to a retreat center to finish the class.

I stayed in the home of an older single woman. She had a one-bedroom apartment. I slept on a sofa in the living room. I ate breakfast and sometimes dinner with her. She had a small water heater and, according to the custom, she turned it on only when she needed hot water for a shower or to wash dishes. She knew maybe ten words of English, much better than my four or five words of Russian. We had some interesting conversations!

I ate lunch in the homes of my credit students. A time or two I had dinner with one of the missionary families living in Kherson. I'm not hard to please with my diet, and I will try almost anything I'm asked to eat. But the Ukraine was a trying dietary experience! It wasn't because of food I didn't like or poorly prepared food; it was the volume of cucumbers I had to consume. Cucumbers were ripe, in abundance, and inexpensive, elevating then to the food of choice for everyone. More days than not I was served cucumbers for breakfast, lunch. and dinner! I like cucumbers —but not that well! By the time I returned to the States, I wasn't sure I ever wanted to see another cucumber again.

The public week of the class was held in a large meeting room on the university campus. It seated about sixty. When we had to go the restroom, we used the reeking, filthy bathroom in the building. The Ukrainian custom was to place used toilet paper in a pail in the bathroom stall, not to flush it. Imagine the stench!

We met each morning 9:30-12:30 for class, followed by a two-hour lunch break. These public classes were popular: the room was filled every day. I had quite a variety of students for this class in child development and ministry. What they didn't know was appalling! For example, a doctor in the class had no idea what the average size of a baby is nor that very young children can learn. Teachers were unaware of any of the developmental material describing cognitive growth in children. Sunday School teachers knew no other way to teach other than to force the children to be seated to listen to them tell everything that was to be learned. Surely these sessions enlightened a doctor, a teacher, a Sunday School teacher or a parent.

On Saturday afternoon I went to a missionary family's home where we enjoyed a good time together. That evening we attended the services for the older church. It was most important that I attend both churches while I was there to avoid any hint of favoritism for one church over another.

The church service proper was prefaced with a half hour or so of Scripture reading. This was a throwback to previous days when they couldn't own a Bible. It permitted people to hear the Word of God even if they couldn't hold it in their hands. The service itself featured enthusiastic singing, passionate prayer, and three sermons. The church would hold another service on Sunday morning, but 80-90 were present that evening.

On Sunday morning, I attended the new church. It met in a movie theater. It was filled this particular morning. The morning was quite a different experience than the evening before. The music was mostly contemporary Christian choruses translated into Russian. Though Scripture was read, it related to the sermon for the day rather than cover some extended section of the Bible. It too was an uplifting worship experience.

On Sunday afternoon the half dozen credit students and I made our way to the retreat center on the Dneiper River outside Kherson, where we would have a couple of hours of class that evening followed by all day Monday, Tuesday and Wednesday and until noon on Thursday. This retreat center was extremely rustic (and that may be too elegant a word to describe it). The male students stayed in one cabin, the females in another, and I in the third. A fourth cabin served as a classroom—a very impromptu classroom at best. There was a restaurant on the grounds where our meals were served morning, noon, and night. Though the conditions were not ideal, we had a productive time together.

On Thursday we returned to Kherson, I again to the lady's apartment where I had stayed the previous week. On Friday, I was transported back to Odessa, this time on a bus for the missionaries to use to transport a mission work group from the States back to Kherson. After the flight back to Vienna, I was happy to discover no cucumbers in my diet for a time.

I went back to the Ukraine five years later. By this time the two churches, and some others that had been planted since I was there before, had cooperated to begin the Tavariski Christian Institute. The original new church plant had grown rapidly and had secured facilities that served both the church and the college.

I stayed in one of the dormitory rooms used by the college—and had to use coeducational shower facilities. The room had a small refrigerator so I could keep some fruit in my room. I needed it, for our meals were sparse. We ate in the college cafeteria. Breakfast was hot milk with a bit of macaroni in it one day, a barley cereal with lots of butter and sugar to put in it the next morning. Lunch consisted of two or three ounces of some kind of meat and a vegetable. The evening meal meant borscht or a repeat of the breakfast pasta and cucumbers, maybe one or two thin slices per person. If it hadn't been for a bit of fruit and some energy bars I had taken with me, I would have been very hungry! As it was, I lost weight that week.

When I arrived in Odessa on my second trip into the country, my luggage didn't arrive with me. I had a bag with a couple of changes of clothes, a toothbrush, class notes, and my Bible. But the other bag—the one that didn't come—had several necessities, some clothes, and a large amount of children's teaching materials that I was leaving with the students. Air Austria said they would deliver my luggage when it arrived, presumably the next day.

Sunday afternoon I had a phone call from Odessa. My luggage had arrived, they said, but I would have to come to Odessa to pick it up. Why the change? Because there was something suspicious in the luggage, they claimed. I told them I could not come. I finally said, "I can list everything in that piece of luggage. Can you tell me what is suspicious about women's underwear and children's teaching material?" I knew by this time that this was a classic Ukrainian scam. If I or anyone else had gone for the bag, we would have had to pay a large bribe to get it. So I finally said, "Look, I'm not coming. And I have no one to send. You said you would bring it. You have my permission to break the lock to confirm what is in it. If you won't do that, store the bag and I'll pick it up Saturday on my way out of the country." The bag was delivered the next day, the lock intact!

I had twenty or so in this class. It went quite smoothly. One interesting observation emerged from the final oral exam. One question asked the students to trace influences in their life (based on the material we had covered) that had profoundly affected them. The majority of the students had been reared in homes where the father was an alcoholic and/or had abandoned them, leaving certain marks on their lives, but also giving them openness to Christianity. Many of these students had a passion for children's ministry, for they knew what a difference it could make in a child's life.

My final trip to the Ukraine was in the early 2000s. Class went well, and I had a good week there. The most surprising thing was running into a former student who was there on a short-term mission trip. On Sunday morning at breakfast I saw a couple in the cafeteria who were very American. I conversed with them briefly and learned that they were from First Church of Christ in Burlington, Kentucky. I mentioned that a former student of mine was on their church staff. They knew immediately who I meant. "Oh, Tommy is here with us," they said. "We will let him know you are here." Tommy Baker and I had a great visit and enjoyed the surprise meeting in another corner of the world!

What is Ukraine's future? It surely has been politically and economically unstable. The Ukraine is very large and is the home of distinct factions, some of them still quite sympathetic to Russia. But the churches seem to be vibrant and focused. Many new churches have been established; new leaders have been educated at both the undergraduate and graduate levels. Barring some unforeseen opposition to Christianity, the churches would appear to have a productive future as they have devoted themselves to evangelism while still reaching out to meet social needs such as homes for children, job creation through cooperative enterprises, and distribution of clothing, food, and medicine to those in need.

Romania

Romania is hard to describe, for the written description varies, depending on what part of the country is featured. My first trip was in 1994, which I descried in some detail in an earlier chapter. Western Romania has something of a rural flavor about it, despite the fact that it was once a tourist haven. It has its share of cities, but traveling the roads may bring you upon an ox cart going to market, a wagon pulled by mules or horses, another pulled by a tractor. The sights of travel and dress reveal a cross section of people representing pre-modernity in clothing and transportation.

Bucharest has quite a different feel to me. It is a large city, the capital of the country, featuring the grand and the slums. Though one would surely find poverty and hunger in rural areas and in the slums, the look of Bucharest reflects a busy, at least semi-prosperous place. If your choice is pizza, it can be found at the Pizza Hut in the center of the city. If you prefer a Big Mac, McDonald's will care for your yen. I have been to Bucharest three times to teach, so I have far more impressions of the city than I do the resort area where I first taught.

Classes in Bucharest met in a teaching center added to a church led by Oti Bunaciu, the TCM national director in Romania and also a professor of theology at the Baptist seminary that has an arrangement for students to also study at the University of Bucharest. The church is very near the slums and has carried out good ministry among the slum dwellers, many of them gypsies. They have operated a school that ministered to slum children to teach the educational basics. They have built space in the slums to house the school and a church and to serve as a center for activities. They would tell you that it has been extremely hard work that they wish had yielded greater dividends. That is undoubtedly so. But at the same time, they have carried out ministry where not many dare to tread.

Two Romanian students and I

The church added sleeping rooms, a small apartment for guest professors, and a kitchen and dining area that serves the slum children in the school and meets the needs of the church and TCM. They added a classroom, this with the help of TCM. The guest apartment was stocked with cheese, bread, deli meats, and fruit so I could prepare my own breakfast. Lunch and dinner were common meals for students and professor, however.

I always had good sized classes in Romania, never less than 18-20, in Bucharest. We had quite good translators. The first one I had in Bucharest was a young woman in her early 20s. She had never taken a formal class in English, but learned the language via television and movies. In fact, she translated for me twice. The third time I was there was at the time of her marriage—and I was privileged to attend her wedding.

I very much appreciated the worship services of the church. The services were somewhat traditional, but full of life. The Sunday evening service was quite a contrast to the morning service. Singing was accompanied by a mandolin choir. The choir always presented a couple of special music presentations each Sunday evening.

I was able to visit landmarks in Bucharest—the government palace built by Coceascu on a wide avenue through part of the central city. He was determined to make Bucharest a Paris of Romania. I saw a folk museum that was reopened after many years. I visited an orthodox seminary and browsed the book shop. Unfortunately, I saw a bevy of "ladies of the night" clustered alongside a major highway attempting to lure truck drivers—and they weren't waiting for night. But by far the most interesting thing I did was to attend the translator's wedding.

I had been to a wedding dinner in Moldova (more about that later), but not the wedding. I was curious enough to want to experience the whole event. Even then, I couldn't experience the entire event, for in Romania a couple must be married in a civil ceremony. Christians can, of course follow that with a Christian wedding. The civil ceremony was on Thursday, the Christian wedding on Saturday.

I arrived at the wedding and went to the balcony to sit. That didn't last long, however. I was fetched by someone who said that I, as a guest of honor, must sit in the second row with the pastor's wife. The wedding featured a wedding processional with the couple and their two attendants, one for each the bride and groom. The wedding consisted of music and three sermons—one by the groom's pastor, one by the bride's father who was associate minister of the church where the wedding was held, and one by Oti, the pastor. Rather than guests bringing gifts, an offering was taken during the ceremony to give to the couple.

The wedding feast followed. The couple had very much wanted to be non-traditional and dispense with the wedding feast and replace it with an American-style cake and punch reception. But her parents wouldn't hear of such action, for, they said, people would think they were trying to be penny pinchers and withhold the proper social amenities from guests.

And was it a feast! Meats, salads, vegetables—and many different dishes of each—plus cake, and soft drinks, coffee, lemonade, tea! It was quite a warm day so cold soft drinks were consumed by the gallon. Guests made trip after trip to the buffet table. No one needed anything else to eat that day.

The church in Romania has been strong, formed because of the persecution and deprivation of the long Communist period. Some leaders worry a bit that the church has become soft in recent years. Though the church is still strong in outreach, growth is actually slower now than it was under Communism. That said, some extremely large churches, by anyone's standards, have emerged. Some outstanding younger leaders have been well educated, are zealous for ministry, and have a deep commitment to their call. Romania is the country with the largest number of students enrolled in the TCM Institute. One would expect to see God move even more strongly in this place.

Moldova

Many Americans have never heard of Moldova. It is a small landlocked country in Eastern Europe, located between Romania to the west and Ukraine to the north, east and south. Moldova was a part of the United Soviet Socialist Republic until that disintegrated when most of the republics forming the U.S.S.R. broke off from the motherland and formed their own governments. The capital of Moldova is Chisinau where we conducted classes.

The church in Moldova is an active church with a long outreach into the "Stans" of central Asia. A Christian college has been established to train leaders for Moldova and the "Stans." Each year Mihail Malancea, the Dean of the school, makes a trip to places like Kazikstan or Uzbekistan to recruit twenty students to go to Moldova to study for two years with the purpose of going back to the home country to evangelize. The top students are invited to stay at Chisinau Christian College to complete a degree program before they return home permanently. The top graduates are encouraged to do graduate study at the TCM Institute. Mihail is gaining some reputation as an authority in Muslim evangelism and has done a Ph.D. in that area through the University of Bucharest.

My first trip to Moldova was in the early 2000s. I flew to Budapest and then another flight to Chiseneau. The city was served by a new modern airport, something of a surprise to me. Chiseneau is not a large city, but, like many Eastern European cities, it is marked by wide avenues for the main thoroughfares, high rise apartments and a minimum of green space. I actually saw little of the city during my three visits there.

Come Travel with Me

Chisineau Christian College occupies one multi-story old building which houses the library, some classrooms, offices, the college cafeteria, and rooms and apartments for students and some staff. The very small campus has a more recently built structure used for a variety of purposes and another small building. I stayed in a third floor staff apartment that had a stocked refrigerator, allowing me to eat breakfast in my own quarters each day.

I arrived on Saturday. On Sunday I was scheduled to speak at the church where Mihail preaches. They were in the midst of building a new home for the church and had a sizable room finished enough for the congregation to meet to worship. The space was filled that morning.

Mihail explained that we would be going to a wedding feast as soon as we left the worship service. One of the faculty members at the college was getting married that morning. The wedding was during the church service at another congregation so we would miss the wedding, but we would be at the feast.

What an interesting afternoon I spent! We arrived at the college where the feast was being held about noon, a little ahead of the newly married couple. The college cafeteria was filled to overflowing. When the newlyweds arrived, they and their attendants were escorted to the head table which had been elevated to make it possible for all the guests to see them. A master of ceremonies then took over. He kept the afternoon running smoothly. Now and then he invited people to participate: some read poetry; others gave pieces of advice. A band provided music in between the speaking.

And we ate! Every inch of the table was covered with food. Everyone ate heartily from the delicious cold dishes on the table. I supposed this was the whole of the food for the occasion. But wrong, absolutely wrong. Soon the original dishes were removed and hot food took its place, again every inch of the table covered. After another hour or so, the wedding cake was served. All through the meal mineral water and drinks were available. It was an exceptionally hot day so many bottles of drinks were consumed.

Mihail told me that I need not feel compelled to stay until the dinner was finished and other guests were leaving. About 3:30 p.m. I took my leave. I could hear the band and the festivities in my apartment—and they went on until after 6:00.

I had about twenty students in class, some of them exceptionally capable. My translator was a young Moldovan woman who had finished college in Iowa. She was excellent, and we worked very well together. I would have loved to have had her again but that didn't happen on either of my next two trips to the country. She immigrated to the United States, one more in a steady brain drain from Moldova.

The second Sunday I was there I was a guest in Mihail's home for dinner, along with several other guests. I think I have never been in a home as happy as that one appeared to be. He and his wife had two teenage children, two of the most polite and friendly teenagers I've ever met. But the darling of the family was Emmy, a precocious two-year-old who was the apple of everyone's eye. It was a delightful time of fellowship—and besides that, Lydia cooked very well. They entertained me for a meal every time I was in Chiseneau.

The second time I went to Moldova, I had three or four students from Asia. One was from Azerbaijan, the others from Kazikstan. I visited a great deal with the young men from Kazikstan. The class was on small group leadership.

One day he expressed concern. As a way of demonstrating how to form small groups, I had the class divided into small groups that spent time in prayer and Bible study each day. His concern? How practical was this for him in his ministry? In his country people didn't sit in chairs in study groups but rather sat on cushions on the floor. He didn't question anything else, but he was afraid I was teaching them to do something culturally irrelevant. I assured him that he could apply the principles however a group was seated, and he was satisfied. This same young man was so devoted to his studies that he rode the train for five days to get to Chiseneau—and, of course, would have to ride five days to get home. He was an inspiration to me.

My final trip to Moldova went as well as the first two. I had eighteen to twenty in my class Principles of Teaching and uncovered some outstanding storytellers in the group. The highlight of that trip was a tour of the countryside outside Moldova with Mihail, Emmy, and another TCM professor who had just finished a class and would leave the next day. We saw many old Roman ruins and the buildings of several churches. The day was capped off with a visit to a pizza restaurant.

My translator was Mihail's nephew who was a student at the university. He was a bright, capable young man who had aspirations that he wasn't sure he could achieve, not because of lack of desire, effort, or talent, but because of the corruption of the university system. To do what he hoped to do required not only top grades, but a rank at or near the top of the class. He did well on his exams but was unable to reach the needed ranking because he refused to pay the bribe most professors demanded of those who received the top rankings. It was obviously a grossly unjust system, but one so deeply ingrained in the university system that it gave him little promise of changing. I've often wondered what happened to that young man. Did he join the brain drain leaving the country?

Moldova is such a tiny country but the home of many churches, both older and newer. Chiseneau Christian College seems to have been a catalyst to focus the churches on their unique position to be an evangelistic force into central Asia to former Soviet dependencies. It is an incredible opportunity, for Moldovans can travel freely to these countries on their Russian passports, and the central Asians can travel freely to Moldova. It is an opportunity that could be removed in the future, but for the time being, Moldova can be an entryway into Muslim lands for evangelism.

Bulgaria

My first trip to Bulgaria, described earlier, was in 1992. It had been perhaps a decade since anyone from TCM had been able to enter the country until Vanita Dulin and a friend went in 1990. Even then, they were followed by the authorities and were unable to make much meaningful contact with any Christian leaders. But by 1992, contact had been re-established and a teaching week planned. To fulfill those plans was my purpose for being there.

Once classes were credit bearing, I made three more trips. The first of these three trips took us back to Velingrad to the Holiday House for Miners. I had about a dozen in the class. I remember that it was during the World Cup playoffs and that the Bulgarian team was a strong contender. We planned much of our schedule around the times the Bulgarian matches would be televised. And, of course, I was cheering for Bulgaria along with the students!

My last two trips moved the class site closer to Sophia at a resort high on a hill above the city. Each class had fifteen to eighteen enrolled. The hotel was a good venue: it was spacious, accommodating us and other guests as well; provided comfortable facilities, though simply furnished; served excellent food; and was near the city and airport. The staff was quite accommodating, making it a pleasant place to stay. It was there in 2001 that I discovered the recurrence of the eye problem that eventually led to my legal blindness.

It is somewhat difficult to speculate about the future of the Bulgarian church. I attended only two different churches in the country, the one in Velingrad led by the two young women and a Methodist church in Sophia that had been re-opened after the return of its property after the fall of Communism. The first seemed to be a dynamic congregation, but the second didn't. I came across no churches of any size represented by students enrolled in my classes. At the same time, I was most impressed by the students who had a zeal for ministry and a desire to see the church strong in their country.

Czech Republic

I have always had a fondness for the Czech people. I met a group at the Haus in 1990 when I first visited TCM. They were friendly, open, happy people who made it a joy to be around them. I always tried to position myself at a table with some of them at mealtimes.

I didn't make it to the Czech Republic until 1997. I went to Europe about ten days before my TCM class was scheduled to meet. I had been invited to be a part of a conference on ministering to youth that was being conducted in Bruno. Someone from that city drove to the Haus to transport me to the home of Frank and Mila Markov. Mila and I had become friends at the Haus; Frank was pastor at the church where the conference, sponsored by Trans World Radio, would be held. The conference was an all-day Saturday event, attended moderately well. It was a receptive group. That evening I taped several interviews that would later be used on Trans World Radio. On Sunday, I worshiped at Frank and Mila's church before someone took me back to Vienna on Monday.

My second trip was the following year. I spent a few days at the Haus finishing my preparation for the class in Kreb. On Saturday I departed on the train for Prague where I would be met by the Czech field director.

The Czechs were building a teaching center not yet ready to use. I had carried $10,000 in new $20 bills with me to Europe. Now I had to finish the delivery and take the money with me to deliver to the field director.

I boarded the train in Vienna. Four young men were sharing my compartment. My first big surprise was when they stood, stripped off their slacks, and put on walking shorts. The field director met me and took me to a pension to deposit my belongings and freshen up. He returned an hour or so later to take me to lunch and into the central city square where he showed me some of the sights of Prague. We walked over the long Charles River Bridge, watched glassblowers and artisans of all kinds ply their arts, and visited the John Hus museum and church where Hus had made many of his reformation pronouncements that brought down the wrath of the Church on his head. We then met the director's wife and daughter to eat pizza for our evening meal. We cut through the Jewish sector to catch a bus for me to return to my pension. And I gratefully handed over the money to the field director who stuffed it in his inside jacket pocket before going to his home.

The class was held in Kreb, near the German border. The field director, who would translate for me, and I took a train from Prague to Kreb. I stayed in an old, but nice pension about six blocks from the church, a nice walk a couple of times a day. The pension featured a hearty European breakfast. We had class from 8:30 to 12:30 each day followed by our noon meal that had been prepared by the ladies of the church. We had an afternoon break. After dinner back at the church, we met for three hours.

The class was small—perhaps ten in number. One of the men in the class was in the original group of Czech I had met in 1990 at the Haus. He explained that his wife wanted to come for the class, but that this was their church's week of camp and she had to be there. He then asked if I would be interested in going to the camp one afternoon if he could find transportation. Of course!

He arranged the transportation for Thursday afternoon. The driver, the field director, he and I made our way to the camp about an hour away. It was being conducted on a farm with a big house, some outbuildings, and plenty of space. As we made our way down the lane into the property, we saw a man and a woman walking toward the house. The others in the car knew them so we stopped to talk. I knew that the occupants of the car were explaining who I was. Just then the man outside the car leaned down and said to me in perfectly good English, "Where in the United States are you from?" I answered, "From Tennessee." "Where in Tennessee?' he inquired. "Johnson City," I replied. He lit up and responded, "I'm from Kingsport." It turned out that he was indeed from Kingsport. He had gone to the Czech Republic to volunteer for a time, met a woman and

Call Me Teacher

married, and stayed on. He and his wife were helping with the camp.

Later in the afternoon, after we had been there for an hour or so, it was time for afternoon break complete with cake and coffee. The man from Tennessee sat at the table with me, and we conversed. "Where do you worship in Johnson City?" he asked. "First Christian Church," I told him. "Oh, the candy kiss church," he answered enthusiastically. "And how is Pastor Mike?" It was another surprise. Come to find out, he was a brother-in-law of the church secretary! It is a good reminder that wherever you go, it is always possible to run into somebody who may know something about you or someone you know.

I taught in the Czech Republic a couple more times in the early 2000s. These classes were held about an hour west of Bruno. This was a rural location, a family farm belonging to the former Czech field director who had died suddenly a year or two earlier. TCM was funding a building on the premises that housed a kitchen, classroom, and sleeping rooms. The widow of the former field director managed the facility when church camps or TCM classes met. It was a good setting for a class—quiet, plenty of space for study and recreation, and conducive to student interaction when classes were not in session.

The first class I taught there was small—only about eight students. However, I had very good students, and we had a good week together. The rural, peaceful setting and small class didn't produce any particularly memorable events.

One of the TCM staff drove me to the class site the second time I taught at the camp. I had perhaps fifteen students in the class. Something unusual occurred this time. We always had a translator available, and it was no different this time. But every student was proficient in English. The translator was rather happy about it: she announced that she was going to sit in the class as a student. She had never been able to do that and seemed to enjoy the experience. That this happened is an indication of how quickly after the fall of Communism English was taught in schools and learned in adult classes all over the country.

Czech has the lowest percentage of Christians of any of the former Eastern European Soviet satellites. Coming out of the Communist era, churches were small and interest in the Gospel by nonbelievers was low. Several young, energetic leaders have emerged, however, and have been educated for ministry. It will be a long-term project to make any significant impact on Czech, but there is some hope for the future.

Hungary

I described my trip to Hungary in some detail earlier. Unfortunately, I never had opportunity to go again, though I did teach one Hungarian class at the Haus. I always enjoyed the Hungarians—they had some excellent students and some outstanding leaders among them. The church where I was in the Balaton region was dynamic and effective. It is my impression that one could find several churches like it. The leaders trained for Hungary were generally beyond middle age in my experience. I have so little knowledge that I can't really make accurate observations.

Poland

Through the years I taught several Polish groups at the Haus, but I didn't make my first trip there until 2003. I flew to Warsaw on a Saturday and stayed at a hotel there until Sunday afternoon. On Sunday morning I attended Pawluska Street Church of Christ in the heart of Warsaw.

The Restoration Movement has a substantial history in Poland. Many of the original churches were located in the east, near what is now Belarus. However, the Pawluuska Street church was among the oldest, if not the oldest Christian church in Poland. The churches had a hard existence during the Communist years, but had cooperated to carry out ministry. They cooperated as they could with the Polish Catholic Church. After 1990, the Christian churches had developed a camp that met a number of needs and served as something of a hub for the churches.

The Pawluska Street church was an active congregation. They met in facilities that were old, but well kept. The worship center was attractive and inviting. The church made the Lord's Supper very much the center of the worship experience. The preaching was certainly quite good, but it was subservient to the celebration of the Lord's Supper.

I attended the second service and the building was nearly full. Judging from the people I saw milling around after the first service, I would suppose it too nearly filled the worship center. They provided translation for English speakers at their services. There would be a third service later in the day, it in English, in a location near the expatriate community. They averaged about five hundred in attendance each weekend, giving them the notoriety of being the largest Protestant church in Poland.

The class was held at the camp, a comfortable place to meet. We had a large classroom. Sleeping quarters were on the second floor of the building and were more than adequate. We ate our meals in the dining room. And the food was delicious. A pool table and other recreational facilities were available for use during free time.

The class was Principles of Christian Teaching. I had twenty enrolled, and with only an exception or two, all of them were motivated, creative, and capable. The students, almost all credit seeking, were pastors, teachers, Christian education leaders from a wide age range. The week was so enjoyable—one of the most enjoyable of my in-country classes—that it seemed simply to fly by.

The churches in Poland have survived, sometimes thrived, through the years. Older Christian leaders have led the church with wisdom. Younger leaders are beginning to emerge. Certainly the church in Poland will survive—and likely do more than merely survive, but instead build on their long history.

Other Eastern European Contacts

I have recounted trips into former Soviet countries to teach. I won't go into detail with other groups I have taught except to mention them. I taught students from all the countries I surveyed at Haus Edelweiss as well, of course. But I've also taught groups from Belarus, Latvia, Lithuania, and Estonia. Interestingly, I've never taught men from Belarus. When Belarussians have come to the Haus to study, the men have always taken another course and left the women to take the teaching courses. Surely it isn't always true, but when I've taught, the women have never taken a Bible or theology course. I suspect this reveals a very conservative group of people with rigid male/female roles and expectations. Anywhere in Eastern Europe is conservative but through class discussions, actions, and attitudes I perceive the Belarussians as the most conservative, and perhaps the most resistant to change.

Mexico

I mentioned earlier three trips to Mexico to attend the annual missionary reunion. Those were good trips, but my contact was with mostly American missionaries. I made a fourth trip in 1997, this time to teach Mexicans.

I spent my entire time working with missionaries, all of whom were at that time aligned with Christian Missionary Fellowship. The first site was Pachuca. There I went two different days to schools to work with kids about bullying that went on in their schools. It was a challenge that I'm not sure I met it very well. The groups were huge, making it difficult to gain and keep attention. The ethos was "kids in control" which didn't help the situation. But seemingly what we did mattered, especially with the younger children. At least it provided a challenge! I also taught a small group of teachers from the church in a single session.

My next stop was Mexico City. There I was the speaker for a women's breakfast attended by women from several churches. It was a lovely event in a nice restaurant, and sixty or more women attended. I also worked with Christian education leaders from a newer church on the north side of Mexico City.

Though I kept busy all week, the major event of the week was a teachers' seminar on Saturday at the north side church. Churches from Mexico City and nearby suburbs attended. It began shortly after noon and extended until early evening with a break for a wonderful Mexican dinner provided by the host church. Close to a hundred attended the event, elating the planners and hosts. The participants were lively and most receptive. It was worth going to Mexico to do, had nothing else I did succeeded.

Philippines

I made two trips to the Philippines in two successive years after I left TCM. On each occasion I went to International Christian College for Ministry in Manila to teach credit courses in this small college led by Ross and Cheryl Wissmann. The college had a few full-time teachers and adequate staff, but depended a good bit on qualified Americans and Australians to teach other courses. They were preparing ministers and teachers for Christian schools. In their short history they have done a commendable job of fulfilling their mission.

I spent three weeks there the first time I went. I taught two classes, one in leadership and the other in teaching skills. Each class had over thirty enrolled. I found the students something of a challenge. For one thing, they were so young. Most Filipino youth graduate from high school at sixteen or seventeen. Conducting a class is even more challenging than teaching college freshmen in the States. Keeping the students focused was a never-ending task. They were a whole lot more interested in the opposite sex than they were about being leaders. Secondly, because of their age, they had little experience to connect to the material, leaving me to come up with illustrations, difficult at best in another culture.

The first weekend I was in the country, I worshiped with one of the local churches led by an ICCM graduate. I had no responsibilities except to worship God. The second weekend Ross Wissmann, a couple of other college staff members, and I went north into a central province where

I conducted a seminar on a state university campus on Saturday morning.

We left on Friday afternoon to go north, arriving in time to eat dinner in the home of one of the trustees of the college. They fed us sumptuously. The trustee was employed by a company that worked with Chinese scientists to develop a better strain of rice. The company had apartments in which the visiting Chinese scientists lived. We occupied a quite comfortable two-bedroom unit that could accommodate the five of us from Manila.

The seminar was held in the chapel of the college. Perhaps forty people from area churches attended, along with a dozen or more university students who were interested in the topic to be sure, but also to fulfill a class assignment. The students insisted on a group picture be taken to record the event. Following the seminar, the trustee and his wife hosted our group at a restaurant on campus, a meal complete with all sorts of Filipino delicacies.

We made our way back to Manila, driving through extremely heavy rain. When we arrived in Manila, much of the city was in darkness. We were close to running out of gas, but couldn't buy any because the stations had no electrical power to pump gas. We finally made it back to the college, finding a gas station just before we got there.

The next morning, I was up bright and early to go to an area church to speak. We were invited to stay after the service to share in a birthday celebration with one of the ladies of the church. (The custom is that the one celebrating provides the food for the party.)

The biggest "extra" event of this trip was a seminar for Christian education leaders of churches in the area. It was scheduled for the third Saturday I was in the country. It was the first venture of this magnitude attempted by the college, and they had worked diligently to make the arrangements and publicize the event. The college provided a meal at noon for all of the participants. Their hard work and prayer were rewarded. The morning of the seminar the excitement was high as people began to arrive. The attendees were attentive and asked insightful questions. At the end of the day, we were informed that one hundred twenty or a few more had been present. What a rewarding day for those who planned so well and worked so hard!

My final Saturday in the country was a free day before returning home. Although heavy rains were occurring daily, Cheryl Wissmann and I traveled to the highlands area outside Manila to do some sightseeing. We visited what was once a government building housing the president of the country for holidays. We enjoyed lunch in a scenic restaurant and good fruit we bought at a roadside stand.

My next trip to the Philippines was the following September. This time I was there for two weeks. I taught two classes, one that met every morning and for a couple of hours in the afternoon. The other met from 6:00 to 9:30 pm each evening. The morning class was very large—sixty students. This time I had motivated, creative students who did excellent work. The second class was a good bit smaller, but with equally good students. I'm not sure why the difference in the maturity and motivation of students from one year to the next, but it was refreshing.

The first weekend I was in the country, personnel from the college and I went south to the original Restoration Movement church established in the country. There I did a workshop for Christian education leaders. This congregation met in a magnificently beautiful building built with white stone and finished with white stone in the interior. The church hosted the seminar participants from area churches for lunch in a restaurant across the street. Approximately forty attended this event that lasted into mid-afternoon.

We drove back to Manila that evening. The next morning, I spoke at an area church not far from the airport. My only sightseeing came that afternoon when I visited the American Cemetery in Manila. It was a somber experience viewing the burial sites for thousands of Americans who lost their lives in the Philippines during World War II.

My final Sunday in Manila took me to another area church to speak.

The Restoration Movement has been active in the Philippines for over a century. Some churches are doing very well; others are ministering less vibrantly. The work is organized throughout the country with an annual national convention, other area and national meetings, publications, orphanages and colleges serving various sections of this country that extends so far from north to south. Some of the institutions are less than effective now, having apparently lived out their life cycle. But replacing them are new leaders and new institutions. The churches celebrated their centennial as a movement a few years ago—and are on their way to another century of service.

India

The country where I have spent the most time is India. In an earlier chapter I described my first trip to India to visit Kulpahar Kids Home. I've never been back to visit, but I made another eleven trips to India, all to the south of the country.

My connection with India began in the fall of 1986 in Cincinnati when an Indian student, new to the seminary, enrolled in a Creative Bible Teaching class I was teaching on Monday evening that fall. I arrived early to set up the classroom the first evening and met the student who was also early. He introduced himself as Abraham Thomas. I could tell him that I had once visited his country, and we struck up a lengthy conversation. During his two-and-a-half years at Cincinnati, we became good friends and I kept in touch with him once or twice a year after he returned home in early 1990. He repeatedly asked me to come to India, but I was never in a position to do it until I moved to Emmanuel in 1994. I had no responsibilities during the Emmanuel Wintersession in January 1995, and I had plenty of frequent flyer miles to buy a ticket. I decided to go. Little did I know what this would mean over the next several years.

For the first trip my flyer miles took me to Delhi where I flew on south to Cochin to meet Abraham. I stayed with him and his family—his wife Valsa and two daughters Sneha, who was ten, and Stefi, who was five. The center for his work was in the mountains of Kerala where he had developed a work among lower caste Hindus. In the five years since his return, he had established three churches and baptized over five hundred, the vast majority converts from Hinduism.

I went to work immediately. Each afternoon about 4:00 pm, Abraham and I would leave to make the three-hour drive up the mountain. We started at an altitude given to rubber plantations, climbed to pineapple plantations succeeded by coffee plantations, and ended up at our destination in the tea plantation area. We arrived at the church where we were to meet about 6:45 pm, and I would begin teaching about 7:00 p.m. Although the church didn't have a permanent electrical source, the leaders had rigged up a temporary source for use each evening. The session ended about 9:30 p.m., and we made the trip back to Abraham's home, arriving at midnight or shortly after. Valsa had food ready. And by that time I was ready for bed!

We made the trip three successive nights before Valsa convinced Abraham that I couldn't do that every day. It's a good thing she did. The first day we didn't go I was absolutely exhausted. I got up at 8:00 am, drank some orange juice, and went back to bed and slept until 3:00 that afternoon. We settled into an every other day pattern, and I was in the mountains seven evenings to teach. And, of course, I was there on Sunday, preaching in two different churches.

The first Sunday was at the first church started by Abraham. The other two churches came also and brought their baptismal candidates. The church building was in a remote location, but after the worship service, we went to an even more remote setting where there was a reservoir of water. Abraham baptized eighty people into Christ that day. Interestingly, at many Indian baptisms, in this region at least, the one being baptized takes on a new name, one found in Scripture.

Baptisms

I was impressed with the work that Abraham was doing. One day I reflected to him that I appreciated his work and wondered how he kept everything moving along now that he had two or three pastors working with him. "I do what you and Dr. Ellis taught me to do," he responded. "And that is?" I asked. "We meet together a day each week. We pray and study. We reflect on what we did that week, and we evaluate it. Then we plan for next week. And we do it." When I reported that to Joe Ellis after I returned, he said, "Imagine that. A student who did what you told him to do!"

Abraham and Valsa lived in a comfortable home, though quite modest. He had built the house while he was working in Saudi Arabia even before he had been in America for his graduate education. He had only a motorcycle for transportation. (We had a car and driver for my trips to the mountains.) And the longer I was there, the more I realized that they were barely subsisting. They had less than a hundred dollars a month financial support from American churches. Abraham had become depressed: his evangelistic work was going so well, but he could not care for his wife and family. He has told me more than once that he was ready to give up the work within months of when I was there.

I couldn't promise financial support, but I did promise him that I would make some contacts on his behalf when I got home. Fortunately, those contacts paid dividends. East 91st Street Christian Church in Indianapolis was quite interested in supporting native evangelists in the 10/40 window and decided to take on the family's living support, an arrangement that exists to this day. First Christian Church in Elizabethtown, Kentucky took on support for special ministry projects. A family, and later their church in Kansas, began to send regular financial support. The Lord raised up those who saved the work of a devoted, able leader.

I didn't go again until late December 1998, returning home in January 1999. This time the teaching was designed to develop the pastors. Several more churches had been planted and pastors employed. However, the majority of pastors had no more than two years of Bible college work, calling for ongoing development for them. Eighteen to twenty pastors gathered every day to study together.

A pastor's class

By this time Abraham had a vehicle. We left on Tuesday morning early and arrived in time for class. We stayed in a third or fourth class Indian hotel. It was shabby at best, but it was clean. We would stay until I finished class at noon on Friday at which time we returned to Abraham's home until Sunday morning when we went to two or three churches where I preached. The next week we followed the same schedule.

Eventually an Indian hotel catering to tourists and businessmen opened, and we stayed there for trips after 1998-99, not even going to Abraham's home. He and Valsa had an apartment in the Center that served as the headquarters for the mission. I almost always ate lunch with them. We adopted a different schedule as well. On Monday, we began class at 10:00 am and took a lunch and afternoon break at 1:00 pm. At 4:00 pm, we reconvened until 7:30 pm. On Tuesday through Friday, we began class at 9:00 am with the rest of the day the same except for Friday when we had no evening session. By the end of a week I knew I had done something!

Through the years we studied Genesis, Hebrews, Gospel of John, Isaiah, Job, Revelation, Prison Epistles, 1 and 2 Corinthians, and children's ministry, among other topics. When we could devote forty to forty-five hours per study, we could deal with a good volume of material.

Pastor's class in 2010

The Anchor class that I taught back in Johnson City became quite interested in this work, especially with the rice distribution to the poor and hungry. Each year they took an offering to buy rice for me to distribute in their names when I was there. They usually sent about four hundred dollars. That sum would buy twelve to fifteen thousand pounds of rice, enough to distribute fifteen pounds to a thousand families. That amount of rice would last the average family about ten days. The people were always deeply appreciative for the food.

Distributing rice

One Christmas when I was there, we did our usual rice distribution. I asked Valsa what Christmas would be like for the people. She said that it would be a bit brighter than usual. Since the families had the rice we had distributed, they could likely buy a chicken as a special treat.

I had sometimes combined my trip to work with Abraham to work with Peter and Cathy Ignatius at Lakeview Bible College and Seminary in Chennai, usually spending a week with them teaching a graduate class. Now and then I would do some work at the English speaking congregation in the city.

A Class at Lakeview

    Peter Is a native Indian who met Cathy, a South African at Cincinnati, They were married while they were students at Cincinnati Bible College and Seminary. When they began work in India they were told by Peter's mentor with whom they intended to work that they were to assume leadership of the Madras College of Evangelism. They did that, but they had dreams far bigger than a three-year Bible institute. They found property on what was then outside the city of Chennai, built a campus, and built a college and seminary that is now accredited by the Asian theological accrediting agency. They have educated many fine ministers who are doing stellar work. I have taught there several times and have gained profound respect for this work and Peter and Cathy's leadership.
    It is the work of the Abrahams, the Peters, and the Cathys that makes me glad that I have been a teacher. And

it provides hope that the Gospel can one day penetrate deeply this mammoth country.

Farewell dinner with faculty

My overseas teaching has presented its fair share of challenges, but it has been such a satisfying experience. I am a far better person for having done it.

Chapter 11

THOSE SLIGHTLY TARNISHED GOLDEN YEARS

Most people move toward retirement with some kind of expectations. I did. I could see myself spending three to four months each year teaching overseas, the rest of the year at home in Tennessee. And it worked that way for two or three years. And then it changed dramatically.

My eyes continued to deteriorate to the point that I began to think of giving up driving. That required a change in living arrangements. Examining the options, I decided I needed to be near family. I found a retirement village in Savoy, IL just minutes from both my sisters in Urbana. I moved there June 27, 2012. It was a good move. Little did I know how much I was going to need to be near family so soon.

On January 22, 2013, I left the States for my annual trek to India. I spent a day and night in Amsterdam before flying to Mumbai where I arrived near midnight the 24th. After two nights there, I flew on to Madurai where I was met by Abraham and a co-worker who took me on to our final destination just into Kerala beyond the Tamil Nadu border.

I preached the first Sunday and taught a week. Though I was sick at my stomach on Friday night, I felt better on Saturday. I assumed I was rid of whatever the malady was. I preached on Sunday, witnessed 91 baptisms, distributed a Bible to each one who was baptized, and distributed rice to about a hundred families. And Monday began my second week of teaching. But when I stood to go to lunch, I could take only three or four steps before I felt like I was going to fall. After lunch I took a nap and felt better. I walked to the bathroom about forty steps away. But once I was in the bathroom, I fell—and I did not walk again until sometime in April.

I supposed that an afternoon of rest would take care of me, so I didn't teach in the evening, but returned to the inn to sleep. But I didn't get better. By noon the next day I asked to go to the hospital, a small Catholic mission facility just outside the town. It had a caring staff, but it became apparent that I needed expertise they could not provide. They transferred me by ambulance to a teaching hospital in Madurai, a seventy-mile ambulance ride away.

I remember arriving in Madurai and perhaps the first couple of hours there, but sometime that Thursday night I went into a coma that lasted until Saturday. The word to my family in the States was that the next twelve hours were critical: if I survived that, I would be able to recover. So began my stay in ICU, thirty days total in that hospital. My diagnosis was urinary tract infection, kidney failure, and pneumonia.

Most Indian hospitals serve no food. It is imperative that a family member or friend provide that part of your care. I was so fortunate that someone from the mission was with me 24/7.

I had an amazing experience, one that I cannot explain. As I was coming out of the coma, I was convinced that demons were fighting with God over my body, the demons trying to draw me into their kingdom, God trying to save me. For a couple of days I experienced this. But it has never occurred again.

The travel insurance arranged for me to return to the States March 1. I was taken to the airport by ambulance. But when I got there, I wasn't permitted to board because the airport had no concourse for boarding, but merely steps which I couldn't climb. Nor had the insurance company arranged with the airline for oxygen. The travel nurse who was accompanying me had oxygen, but airlines must provide the oxygen. Unable to board, we simply went back to the hospital for another week.

I celebrated my 73rd birthday from a hospital bed. But Valsa and the mission personnel invited doctors, nurses, and therapists to eat cake with us. I must have had two dozen well-wishers in and out during the day to enjoy the celebration. One of my doctors who had to be out of town on my birthday came to my room late the night before and brought me a large, colorful birthday card.

A doctor friend, Dr. Binu, who is head of neonatal at a very large teaching hospital in Chennai, kept an active watch on my case. He traveled to Madurai twice to consult with doctors and to reassure me. The doctors and care I received were superior except for therapy. Lung therapy was fine, but I was not out of bed for the time I was at the mission hospital or in Madurai. I became unable to walk. Dr. Binu decided that it would be to my benefit to go to Chennai where he would set me up with the top physical therapist at his hospital. He worked with the travel insurance company to achieve that goal. On March 6, he and

Cathy Ignatius, a former student of mine and close friend of Dr. Binu and his family, flew to Madurai to ride the three hundred miles with me in the ambulance to Chennai.

Once in Chennai, the therapist had me standing the first day and shuffling for two or three steps the second day. We worked at strengthening my responses while Dr. Binu worked with the travel insurance company to get passage to the States. Finally, on March 13, I flew to Chicago, and an ambulance took me to Carle Hospital in Urbana, Illinois, where I remained four days until I was transferred to a rehab facility. I spent seven weeks working hard to be able to walk again.

Back from India and the rehab hospital, I was offered the opportunity to be the pastor for the church that meets in the retirement community and to meet the needs of residents. I accepted. And I found that planning the worship services and preaching each week were quite fulfilling as well as challenging.

But my fulfilling activity came to an end in December. On the night of December 7, I awoke about midnight with labored breathing. I called the desk at our village, and the desk attendant called an ambulance. I was admitted to the hospital with kidney failure and pneumonia. The doctor tried a couple dialysis treatments in the hope that my kidneys would regain function—but they didn't. So I had to go on dialysis permanently. That meant inserting a catheter and doing surgery to put in a fistula. And a new phase of life began.

I left the hospital December 26 and went to the rehab hospital, this time for six weeks, going home February 7. Surely my hardest days were behind me, I concluded. But I was very wrong.

I've done quite well on dialysis itself. But I have had all kinds of problems with related issues. For example, I had a fistula in my right arm. But when it came time to use the fistula in late March, it was determined that my veins were too deep. So in March I had a same-day surgical procedure to raise the veins. The second time it was used, a clot developed. Back to the hospital overnight as they cleared the clot, but couldn't prevent the fistula from collapsing. That called for a surgery in the left arm to create another fistula. The first time it was used my arm was bruised from just below my elbow to the shoulder. I decided then and there that dialysis would always use a catheter. The cardiovascular surgeon concurred. Meanwhile, toward the end of this saga, I had a kidney stone that required an overnight hospital stay. Early in 2015, I fell three times in four days. That put me in the rehab hospital for two weeks to work on balance.

I had been home for less than a week when I broke my leg. It was back to the rehab hospital. At the end of six weeks, I went back to the orthopedist who had ordered a standing x-ray. The technician provided no walker, no assistance of any kind. And I fell, breaking the same leg again. That led to another long stay in the rehab hospital.

I recount all this simply to demonstrate that retirement has not been as I had envisioned. Of course, none of us get to choose our path of aging, particularly our health. Many of my years have been wonderfully golden and satisfying, but long patches of time have had a lot of pain and health troubles, resulting in a good bit of tarnish. However, the years have been given to me to make something of them to glorify God. I've not always been as faithful to this goal as I would like. But I've done the best I can, relying on God to take my inadequate efforts and make something out of them.

Chapter 12

REFLECTIONS

That is it! Seventy-six years reduced to a few pages. What do I make of it? How can this life be interpreted?

I stand firmly on the conclusion that God has directed my life—and in ways I could never have imagined. Despite my own blunders and poor decisions, God has taken every experience to weave a tapestry of His love. I could never have planned these years as they have turned out. I could imagine a few years of youth and educational ministry followed by teaching. But I never could have imagined the variety of experiences that have filled those years. I was interested in missions, but would never have supposed I would teach in the places I have. I could imagine traveling within the United States, but I could never have imagined visiting thirty-five countries of this diverse world or teaching students from twenty-five countries in fifteen different countries of the world. Only God can orchestrate that.

I have carried a good many different titles: youth minister, minister of Christian education, teacher, dean. But I will pick one: just call me teacher.

I have been the first in several areas: the first woman to be a seminary dean (two women had been college deans before I was in seminary), among the first ten women on the NACC planning committee, the first woman on the NACC executive committee, one of the first two women to graduate from Lincoln Christian Seminary, the first woman on the Lincoln faculty to be paid commensurate with the male members of the faculty, the first woman to give the Athearn Lectures at Manhattan Christian College and the Seminary Lectureship at Cincinnati Bible College and Seminary, the first woman to chair the Christian Educators' Conference, the first person to have taught full-time at the three seminaries, the first woman on the staff of four different churches. I never set out to be the first in any of these situations. Only God could have engineered these.

I shake my head when I think of how an extremely shy youngster who had, by age sixteen, been no farther from home than St. Louis about a hundred miles away, who came from a family of modest means, and who had limited means for college and graduate school, has been favored to travel so widely and share with those in many different cultures. Only God could orchestrate that.

I never would have supposed I would live in Oklahoma, Ohio, Michigan, Tennessee, and Austria: Illinois was the farthest I could think. Only God could orchestrate that.

As I am writing this, I cannot foresee, even a little bit, what good can come from a nine-month rehab stay or ending up in a nursing home can result in good. I know I can't make it into something positive. Only God can orchestrate that. And I am waiting on Him for the answer.

So it's been a good life so far. It has borne disappointments, hard times, and discouragement. But those have been far outweighed by the joys and opportunities and relationships along the way. And I have every reason to believe it will be good until I pass to my eternal home. I am confident because God is the same yesterday, today, and forevermore!

Conclusion
by Dr. Bruce Parmenter

I call Eleanor Daniel "The Queen of the Deans" because, to my knowledge, she is the only woman, except Dr. Dinelle Frankland, to serve as academic dean in seminaries of the more "traditional" side of the "Stone-Campbell" fellowship. Eleanor has been Dean at, not one, but three seminaries. She is also a missionary to missionaries and herself a missionary; a scholar par excellence (Summa Cum Laude graduate of Lincoln Christian College, Masters' and Ph.D. from the University of Illinois) and an extraordinary teacher and preacher.

Tucked in among the plethora of Eleanor's gifts, as a kind of lubricant for all the rest, is the gift of friendship. Her roster of life-long friends exceeds the impressive list of books, journal articles, and essays she has written.

Her first published article appeared in the Lookout, "We Recommend Week-Day Church School." This piece was based on the Week Day Church School that Eleanor established at Tuscola, IL, where she served, first as youth minister and later as Director of Christian Education. Years later Eleanor would have a fifteen-year ministry as columnist for the *Lookout.*

Eleanor is author of the book, *Principles of Christian Teaching*, which has been translated into Russian, Romanian, and Polish. Eleanor revised and updated the classic book by Guy Leavitt, *Teach with Success,* since translated into Polish. A 1981 book in the College Press series on *What the Bible Says About*_____, is an encyclopedic treatment of the topic of "Sexual Identity." Scholars researching this subject should have Eleanor's careful and thorough study ready at hand. The following line from the book sets forth both her point of view and her literary style: "Preach God's mercy, repentance as needed, and forgiveness as available."

Through each Deanship she has continued classroom teaching and guidance of student dissertations. She has been a member of teams examining other seminaries for accreditation.

She has also been Director of Christian Education in churches full-time or adjunct to her seminary administration duties.

Eleanor was founder and Director of the Preschool in the Lincoln, IL, Christian Church. That ministry became a thriving program and is still flourishing today.

Eleanor Daniel, the person, is gregarious, laughs often and overflows with a zest for life in spite of loss of vision, multiple fractures, and now on dialysis three times a week. She remains courageously active in "the good fight of faith."

Children and youth have always loved Eleanor, and that may be the highest honor of all. She bonded easily and closely to the young people in the Tuscola church. Notable among those she influenced into ministry is Jim Allison, who taught vocal music at Lincoln Christian University for over forty years.

I was quite surprised to learn from Eleanor that she passed through the first grade without learning to read! It would seem that her first grade teacher did not know how to teach reading, but when Eleanor's resourceful mother discovered the deficiency, <u>she</u> taught her child to read. Eleanor has been reading ever since, and still reads one hundred books a year, with the use of The Talking Books resource. She has a particular interest in biographies of U.S. Presidents.

The Queen of the Deans has preached and taught on three continents, traveling in fourteen different countries (when return trips are added, the total comes to about thirty-five mission trips outside the United States)!

I well remember the series of sermons/lectures in the chapel at Lincoln Christian College in the early seventies on "The Role of Women in the Church." Eleanor gave one of the sermons, and Ron Heine and I also spoke. I say "also" because the male speakers were mere foot soldiers in the sermon parade.

Eleanor was first invited to India by one of her former students at Cincinnati Christian Seminary, Abraham Thomas. On her twelfth trip there she became desperately ill and passed through a near-death experience. Her survival seems miraculous. She returned in a wheelchair to her home in Savoy, IL, where her sisters, Jean and Kay, keep watch over her.

So, the bright youngster with roots in the emphatically rural Pike County, IL, where she was spiritually nourished under the excellent preaching of the pastor of the whole county, Joe Maynard, became a world traveler, distinguished educator, and noted preacher. Now 76 years of age, her life is a powerful testimony for the words of Ephesians 3:20: "Now to him who by the power at work within us is able to accomplish abundantly far more than all we can ask or imagine, to him be glory in the church and in Christ Jesus to all generations, forever and ever. Amen."

About the Author

Eleanor A. Daniel is a retired professor and minister. She knew from the first grade that she wanted to be a teacher. During high school, she felt the Spirit directing that desire toward the teaching ministry of the church. She followed this leading that led in unexpected directions, even to the shadow of the Kremlin. She taught for two years in a church kindergarten and forty years in higher education. She has served as education minister, children's pastor, youth minister, and minister of adult education in congregations in Illinois, Michigan, Oklahoma, Ohio, and Tennessee for twenty years. Her teaching career led her to ten foreign countries to teach. She has also served as a Dean and on accreditation teams for the Higher Learning Commission and the Association of Theological Schools.

She has degrees from Lincoln Christian University (B.A. and M.A.), the University of Illinois (M.Ed. and Ph.D.), with additional work at Central (OK) University and Christian Theological Seminary.

She is retired and living in Urbana, Illinois. She can be contacted at eleanor71@ymail.com.

CPSIA information can be obtained
at www.ICGtesting.com
Printed in the USA
LVOW06s0856020816
498359LV00005B/7/P

9 781498 478465